D1168399

# NUCLEAR WAR

# NUCLEAR WAR

## FROM HIROSHIMA TO NUCLEAR WINTER

## LAURENCE PRINGLE

ENSLOW PUBLISHERS, INC.

| | |
|---|---|
| Bloy St. & Ramsey Ave. | P.O. Box 38 |
| Box 777 | Aldershot |
| Hillside, N.J. 07205 | Hants GU12 6BP |
| U.S.A. | U.K. |

**Library of Congress Cataloging in Publication Data**

Pringle, Laurence P.
    Nuclear war.

    Bibliography: p.
    Includes index.
    Summary: Traces the history of nuclear warfare from the bombings of Hiroshima and Nagasaki to the present situation created by the arms race and predicts the effects of both a limited and a large-scale nuclear war.
    1. Nuclear warfare—Juvenile literature. [1. Nuclear warfare] I. Title.
U263.P73          1985          355'.0217          85-10195
ISBN 0-89490-106-0

Printed in the United States of America

10 9 8 7 6 5 4 3 2 1

**Illustration Credits**
Argonne National Laboratory, pp. 7, 10; Department of Defense, pp. 3, 13, 30, 31, 38, 51, 57, 62, 68, 82, 83; Federal Emergency Management Agency, pp. 44, 76; Food and Agriculture Organization, photo by F. Bottz, p. 73; Food and Agriculture Organization, photo by Jack Ling, p. 98; Laurence Pringle, p. 42; Los Alamos National Laboratory, p. 6; National Archives, p. 91; Office of Technology Assessment, pp. 45, 52, 66; United Nations, photo by Eiichi Matsumoto, p. 47; United Nations, photo by Mitsugu Kishida, p. 48; United Nations, photo by Mitsuo Matushige, p. 105; United Nations, photo by Yosuke Yamahata, pp. 19, 21, 24; United Nations, photo by Yuichiro Sasaki, p. 14; U.S. Air Force, pp. 15, 81; U.S. Department of Transportation/Federal Highway Administration, p. 64; U.S. Forest Service, pp. 17, 101; U.S. Navy, pp. 35, 78.

# Contents

*"Curiosity killed the cat."—ancient proverb*

# 1

# Beginnings

Humans have an insatiable curiosity, a hunger to understand their world. They want to know all sorts of things—how birds fly or why they sing, how matter is held together, or why a star burns.

Seeking answers to the last two questions, scientists found that fires in stars are intimately related to the energy that holds tiny bits of matter together. Star fire is energy emitted when the nuclei of atoms fuse together. The same kind of energy lies within present-day nuclear weapons. More than 50,000 of these warheads are now stored or actually aimed at targets, ready to release their terrible power, ready to burn, maim, and kill millions of people and perhaps even to end human life on earth.

In their worst nightmares, the curious scientists who first investigated the nature of matter never envisioned such a horrible possibility. Among them was Albert Einstein. In a brief report, published in 1905, he suggested that matter is like "frozen" energy and that very small bits of matter are held together by enormous amounts of energy. Einstein, though, had

1

doubts about this idea. To a friend he wrote, "This thought is amusing and infectious, but I cannot possibly know whether the good Lord does not laugh at it and has led me up the garden path."

The actual conversion of matter to energy seemed preposterous, but the idea intrigued nuclear physicists. It also fascinated the author H. G. Wells, who in 1913 wrote a book called *The World Set Free*. In it he forecast the release of nuclear energy and a time of great prosperity resulting from this power source. He also predicted nuclear war, with vast areas left uninhabitable by radioactivity.

In the first third of the twentieth century, research on the atom was dominated by a New Zealand scientist, Ernest Rutherford, who worked in Canada and later in England, and by a Dane, Niels Bohr. Atoms had been thought to be like solid spheres; Rutherford proposed that they were like miniature solar systems, with a core of positively charged protons circled by negatively charged electrons. Niels Bohr refined this model in 1913, explaining how electrons jumped from one orbit to another when an atom emitted or absorbed radiation energy.

Atomic research virtually ceased during World War I as physicists were occupied with studies of aircraft design, antisubmarine devices, and the like. After the war, British physicist Francis Aston conducted experiments that enabled him to estimate the great energy locked within the nucleus of an atom. Aston calculated that the hydrogen in a glass of water, when changed into helium, would yield enough energy to drive a large ship across the Atlantic and back at full speed.

To most physicists, including Einstein, unleashing this power seemed quite unlikely. Aston was more hopeful. In 1925 he wrote, "I have little doubt myself that man will one day be able to liberate and control this tremendous force, and I am optimist enough to believe that he will not devote it entirely to blowing his neighbors to pieces."

Pure curiosity had led to discoveries about the potential energy within atoms, but already there was concern about how humans might use this power. In 1921 Austrian scientist Hans Thirring wrote that it took his breath away "to think of what might happen to a town, if the dormant energy of a single brick were to be set free, say in the form of an explosion. It would suffice to raze a city with a million inhabitants to the ground."

Worry increased as Adolf Hitler came to power in Germany in 1933. This political event had a profound effect on both the pace and the direction of research in nuclear physics. The anti-Semitic policies of Hitler's Third Reich drove many of Europe's finest physicists and chemists to safety in other nations, particularly in the United States. And as the German war machine invaded neighboring countries, scientists became fearful about how new discoveries in physics might be put to use in Germany. War with Nazi Germany loomed ahead, and scientists who normally sought to have their experimental results published and shared with others all over the world became more secretive.

As Germany quickly conquered other European nations, physicists worried that Hitler's scientists would develop nuclear weapons.

There were extraordinary findings to conceal. Late in 1938 two Austrian physicists found that a single neutron (an atomic particle with no electric charge) striking the nucleus of a uranium atom caused it to split apart, or fission, releasing 200 million electron volts of energy. In early 1939 physicists in France and the United States learned that neutrons were also *released* when a uranium-235 atom fissioned. The neutrons thus emitted could strike other uranium atoms, causing them to fission and release more energy and more neutrons, which could strike still other atoms, on and on, in a process called a chain reaction.

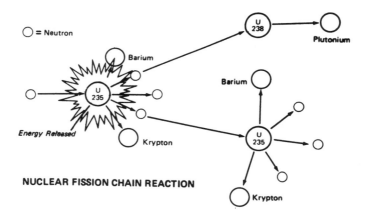

**NUCLEAR FISSION CHAIN REACTION**

This discovery brought humanity a giant step closer to producing nuclear energy. Physicists in several nations, including Germany, began exploring the possibility of starting a nuclear chain reaction. There was still great doubt about the feasibility of wresting energy from atoms, and in 1939 an agreement among a mere dozen scientists to cease work could have delayed for many years the development of nuclear weapons. But World War II was about to begin, and it seemed imperative to press on with efforts to develop nuclear energy and, specifically, a nuclear bomb. In 1939 British physicist and author C.P. Snow wrote, "It must be made, if it really is a physical possibility. If it is not made in America this year, it may be next year in Germany."

So it was made, in America. Although Albert Einstein was less optimistic about nuclear energy than other physicists, he grew increasingly concerned about reports of research in Germany. Encouraged by colleagues, in April 1940 he wrote to President Franklin D. Roosevelt, urging a greater effort in nuclear research. His letter coincided with the German invasion of Denmark and Norway, and the United States soon showed great interest in nuclear experiments. The Japanese attack on Pearl Harbor in 1941 brought the United States directly into World War II and also brought money, materials, and manpower to the Manhattan Project, as the nuclear weapon research program was called.

Unbeknownst to the Americans, British, and other allies, nuclear research was not progressing well in Nazi Germany. The German invasion of the Soviet Union had the further effect of virtually halting nuclear studies in Russia. In 1942, however, a Russian physicist, visiting a university library, noticed a lack of reports about nuclear fission in British and American scientific journals. There were also no articles by most of the world's prominent physicists. From these clues, the scientist concluded that he should urge the Soviet State Defense Committee that "no time must be lost in making a uranium bomb."

The Soviet scientist had guessed correctly: physicists in the United States were hard at work on a vital test of the feasibility of producing a nuclear chain reaction. A team of scientists led by Enrico Fermi was ready to try it by the summer of 1942. The experiment was to be conducted in a specially built structure in a forest 25 miles from Chicago, but completion of the building was delayed, so Fermi obtained permission to use space beneath the football stands at the University of

Chicago. In early December 1942, after many weeks of preparation, the scientists had acquired and assembled the necessary materials.

What they built was called, simply enough, "the pile." Blocks of graphite, uranium, and uranium oxide were arranged in layers within a wooden framework. Thin long rods of cadmium were inserted in deep slots within the pile. Cadmium absorbs neutrons, and these rods were used to slow or halt fission of the uranium nuclei in the pile. As the pile grew, layer by layer, the physicists measured the numbers of neutrons emitted. By the night of December 1, 1942, the pile was about 16 feet tall, and the neutron count indicated that they had reached the necessary amount of uranium—the critical mass—needed for a chain reaction to occur. The cadmium rods were inserted for the night.

Enclosed by wooden boards, the "pile" stood sixteen feet tall when its uranium produced the first humanmade nuclear chain reaction.

The team of scientists present at the chain reaction in 1942; leader Enrico Fermi is on the left in the first row.

The following morning the entire scientific team (fourteen men, one woman) was present for the long-awaited test. Some of the cadmium strips were withdrawn from the pile, and the neutron-counting devices (Geiger counters) began to click. As more control rods were removed, the clicks merged into a steady roar. Only one cadmium rod remained in the pile. Several men stood ready to halt the fission if necessary. One held an ax and waited for an order to chop a rope that held a cadmium rod above the pile. Three others stood on a platform above the pile, ready to flood it with a cadmium-salt solution if the control rods failed to stop the chain reaction.

Enrico Fermi ordered the final control rod withdrawn, bit by bit, during the day as the scientists paused to measure the neutrons. Geiger counters were no longer adequate in counting neutrons; the rapidly increasing numbers of neutrons were recorded by a pen tracing on a revolving paper cylinder. About 3:30 P.M. the remaining cadmium rod was withdrawn one last foot out of the pile, and the pen traced a steady line upward. Fermi raised his hand and announced, "The pile has gone critical."

Humans had lit their first nuclear fire. Fermi let the chain reaction continue for a few moments, then said, "Zip in," and the control rods quickly cooled the pile. Months earlier one of the scientists had bought a bottle of wine for the occasion. Now the wine was poured into paper cups, and everyone drank a toast.

A center for nuclear weapons research was soon set up at Los Alamos, New Mexico. Hundreds of scientists and engineers worked on the secret project. Some joined it reluctantly, their consciences troubled by the potential destructiveness of an atomic bomb. Most, however, believed that, in the words of historian Alice Kimball Smith, "the project would almost certainly end the war and afterwards promised almost limitless benefits to mankind. Amidst the fears and uncertainties of the winter of 1942 and 1943 . . . what more could one ask?"

There was also that powerful human curiosity—would a nuclear weapon explode or fizzle?—and a desire to contribute to a major event in history. Work continued, progress was made, and the actual test of a nuclear weapon became increasingly likely.

By the fall of 1944 the United States government knew that the Germans had made little progress toward nuclear weapons, but scientists working on the Manhattan Project were not told. One recalled: "To the last day of the European war, we were living in constant apprehension as to their [the Germans] possible achievements." Hitler's Third Reich collapsed in May 1945. With Hitler dead and the Japanese losing conquered territory in the Pacific, scientists and others began to question whether or how a nuclear weapon should be used.

President Roosevelt himself had raised these questions in a 1944 meeting, and physicist Leo Szilard, concerned about a postwar nuclear arms race, was scheduled to discuss the matter with the president in the spring of 1945. But Roosevelt died suddenly, and his successor, Harry Truman, rejected suggestions that atomic bombs be demonstrated but not actually used in war.

Through hindsight, it now seems that a nuclear arms race was inevitable once the first nuclear weapon was exploded— whether in war or in a harmless demonstration. In 1945 the only remaining "secret" of the atomic bomb was whether it would work. As physicist James Frank then wrote, "The race for nuclear armaments will be on in earnest not later than the morning after our first demonstration of the existence of nuclear weapons."

The first bomb was ready in July 1945. The test, code-named "Trinity," had been planned for several weeks, and a remote area at Alamogordo Air Base, New Mexico, had been selected as the test site. On July 12 the bomb was carried by truck from Los Alamos to Alamogordo, and the next day it was hoisted to the top of a 100-foot steel tower. As test preparations neared completion, many still doubted that the bomb would work. Some hoped it wouldn't. Enrico Fermi wondered aloud, half jokingly, whether the chain reaction would ignite the earth's atmosphere, destroying New Mexico—or perhaps the entire earth.

Just before dawn on July 16, 1945, all workers were in shelters thousands of yards from the bomb. The last few minutes and then seconds were counted off. A signal was sent to the bomb's detonators. It exploded.

The desert was touched by a searing light, visible nearly 200 miles away. The sky seemed to crack with the force of the explosion. The bomb's steel tower was gone, evaporated, and a 1,200-foot-wide crater marked its site.

"Trinity"—first explosion of a nuclear weapon, in New Mexico on July 16, 1945.

Some viewers laughed, some cried, but most were silent. General Leslie Groves, head of the Manhattan Project, said, "This is the end of traditional warfare." And chemist George Kistiakowsky, who had made the conventional explosives used to detonate the bomb, said, "I am sure that at the end of the world—in the last millisecond of the Earth's existence—the last human will see what we saw."

"I made one great mistake in my life, when I signed the letter to President Roosevelt recommending that atom bombs be made."
—*Albert Einstein*

# 2

# The First Nuclear War

Beginning in April 1945, a committee of scientists and Army Air Force officers studied possible atomic bomb targets in Japan. Their main goal was to impress the Japanese government that defeat was inevitable and thus achieve a quick surrender. Knocking down a great forest would not suffice, they decided; a city with arms-making industries and workers' homes would be the best target. Another goal was to learn more about the effects of nuclear weapons. Therefore, the targets had to be relatively untouched by conventional explosives used in previous air raids.

The target list was short, partly because more than 60 Japanese cities had already been bombed by flights of American B-29s. In July 1945 alone, 43,000 tons of bombs were dropped on Japan. Two raids with incendiary bombs had killed a quarter of a million people in Tokyo. Unbombed parts of Tokyo were ruled out for fear of harming the Japanese emperor. Kyoto, an industrial center, was listed by the target committee, but was removed because this ancient capital was held in such reverence by the Japanese. Hiroshima took its place on the list. Other potential targets were Kokura, Niigata, and Nagasaki.

The decision to drop the bombs on cities is still controversial. United States intelligence had broken the code used in Japan's secret diplomatic messages, and during the summer of 1945 these communications revealed that Japan was eagerly seeking help from the Soviet Union in working out peace terms. But the unconditional surrender demanded by the United States and its allies was resisted by the Japanese, who wanted their emperor to retain his throne.

The apparently desperate straits of the Japanese were known only to President Truman and other top officials in the United States government, who weighed that information against other evidence. The invasion of Japan had been planned and was scheduled to begin in the fall of 1945. Defeat of the Japanese, it was estimated, would take a year, with perhaps a million casualties on each side. The United States had already experienced the fanatic resolve of Japanese kamikaze pilots and knew that surrender was opposed by Japanese military leaders. In early June the Japanese Cabinet had approved a defense plan that called for "100 million people to arise from the vantage ground of their sacred land to strike the invaders dead."

In late June a new Japanese government was formed, and its Cabinet began to seek a negotiated peace settlement. Even so, a July 26 surrender ultimatum from the United States and its allies was rejected by the Japanese. Knowing that the first use of nuclear weapons was imminent, seventy Manhattan Project scientists and engineers signed a petition, urging the president not to use the bomb unless the Japanese were told of its power and still refused to give up. This petition and petitions from other scientists against use of the bomb on Japanese cities never reached the president. Even if they had, President Truman probably wouldn't have changed his mind. He and his closest advisors believed that more than peace with Japan was at stake.

Flights of B-29s had bombed most Japanese cities before the *Enola Gay* carried its nuclear weapon to Hiroshima.

---

They wanted to make the rising superpower of the Soviet Union "more manageable" and believed that use of this extraordinary new weapon would accomplish that goal.

Since August 1, two nuclear weapons had been ready on little Tinian Island in the western Pacific, a 1,644-mile flight from Hiroshima. In the early hours of August 6, a weather observation airplane left the Tinian air base and was soon followed by a B-29 bomber named *Enola Gay* and two other B-29s equipped with cameras and radiation-measuring devices. The first aircraft found fair weather over Hiroshima and reported this fact to the B-29s following.

The *Enola Gay* held a single 4-ton nuclear device containing 12 pounds of uranium. At 8:15 A.M., directly over Hiroshima, the bomb was released and descended by parachute. It exploded about 2,000 feet aboveground. A blue-white flash lit Hiroshima, then a tremendous blast demolished most of the city. American scientists had estimated that 20,000 Japanese would die, but 70,000 perished instantly, and within a few months an estimated 130,000 were dead.

A damaged wristwatch found in the ruins of Hiroshima, stopped at 8:15 a.m. when the bomb exploded.

Damage was so great that communication difficulties kept details from reaching Tokyo for three days. Meanwhile, another nuclear weapon, containing a few pounds of plutonium, was readied on Tinian Island. On August 9 it was carried to Japan in a B-29 called *Bock's Car*. The target: the coastal city of Kokura. As *Bock's Car* flew over Kokura, the bombardier looked for his aiming point—a military arsenal—but industrial pollution and smoke from a large fire hid it from view. Twice more the B-29 flew over Kokura, but the assigned target couldn't be seen.

*Bock's Car* was low on fuel. The captain decided to try the alternate target, Nagasaki. With the fuel remaining, only one pass over the city would be possible. At Nagasaki, clouds also hid the assigned aiming point. Then, through a slight gap in the clouds, the bombardier saw a recognizable target, made some quick bombsight adjustments, then released the 4.5-ton bomb.

It fell for forty seconds beneath its parachute. In the words of a British writer, "And in the forty seconds every move that people chose to make below became of vital importance, a choice between life and death, between degrees of pain and grief."

At 11:02 A.M. the bomb exploded over Nagasaki. About 30,000 people died instantly. The next day the Japanese government offered to surrender. As peace terms were negotiated, some Japanese officers planned a coup and sought to capture a recording the emperor had made announcing surrender to the

*Opposite*: A mushroom-shaped cloud rose over Nagasaki after the plutonium bomb exploded.

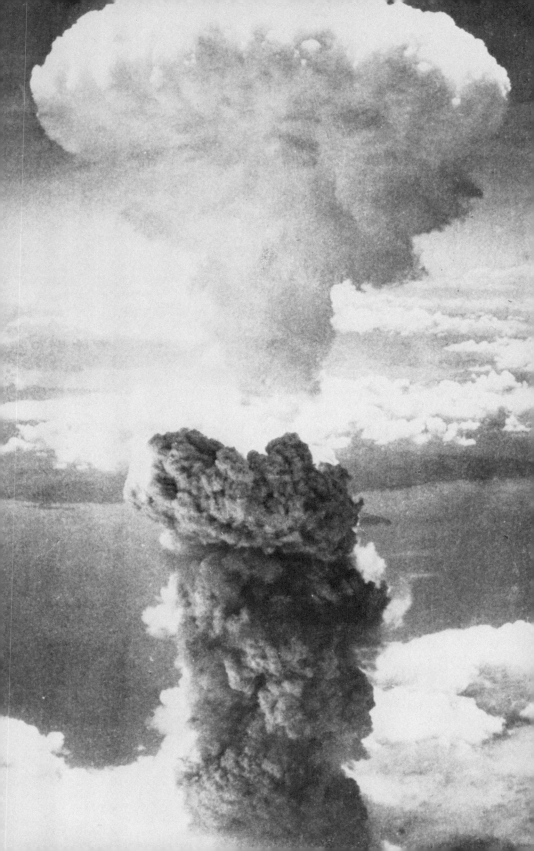

Japanese people. The coup failed, the recording was broadcast, and the first nuclear war was over.

As nuclear wars might go, this wasn't much—two rather small weapons used by one side. But we have learned a great deal about the effects of nuclear arms from Hiroshima and Nagasaki, and some of this knowledge helps us understand what another nuclear war might be like. There are still gaps in our knowledge, though. We will never know, for example, exactly how many people died in the first nuclear war.

Part of our understanding of this nuclear war came long after the explosions in Japan, especially from bomb tests in the American desert and on Pacific islands, which revealed more about the blast, heat, and radiation of nuclear arms.

Until the nuclear age, the most powerful bombs were made of trinitrotoluene, or TNT. A typical large aerial bomb contained a ton of TNT. A thousand tons of TNT is a kiloton, and massive bombing raids during World War II had loosed many kilotons of destructive energy. At Hiroshima, however, a single uranium bomb released 13 kilotons of energy, and the plutonium bomb that devastated parts of Nagasaki yielded 22 kilotons—22,000 times more energy than produced by a single large TNT bomb.

Although we continue to express the power of nuclear weapons in terms of tons of TNT, this ignores characteristics of these arms that make them different from, and more deadly than, conventional explosives. Both TNT and nuclear explosions produce a shock or blast wave that spreads rapidly outward in all directions. The blast wave of a 1-ton TNT bomb causes all wooden buildings within about 150 feet to collapse. At Hiroshima the 13-kiloton atomic bomb caused the collapse of all wooden structures within a radius of 1.2 miles. Pound for pound, the fuel of a nuclear bomb is 100,000 times more powerful than a TNT bomb.

A blast wave is a wall of compressed air. As it spreads outward from a nuclear explosion, it is followed by winds of several hundred miles an hour—up to six times the force of a hurricane. The shock wave's force is measured in terms of air pressure. Normal air pressure at sea level is 14.7 pounds per square inch. Nuclear explosions create great overpressures, up to or beyond 20 pounds per square inch above normal.

---

In the 1980 eruption of Mount St. Helens, a blast wave felled thousands of acres of trees. Some trees still stand (left); they were shielded from the overpressure by topography, as were parts of Nagasaki.

Although brick and wooden structures fall apart under an overpressure of 5 pounds per square inch, the human body can withstand higher overpressures without injury. Lungs are damaged at an overpressure of 12 pounds per square inch. People exposed to less overpressure are still likely to die or be injured, however, by being hurled about by the wind, pierced by flying glass, wounded by other flying objects, or crushed by collapsing buildings. Although the force of the blast and its winds lessens with distance, at Hiroshima it was still powerful enough to break windows 16 miles from ground zero—the point on the ground closest to the center of the explosion.

Both TNT and nuclear explosions produce heat or thermal radiation, but while conventional explosives reach about 9,000°F, a bursting nuclear warhead yields heat energy of tens of millions of degrees—the temperature of the interior of the sun. In fact, a nuclear explosion is like bringing a piece of the sun close to the earth. Enormous amounts of this energy are released as an expanding fireball, which reaches its maximum size one second after the explosion. A person whose eyes were actually focused on the fireball would be permanently blinded.

The heat travels at the speed of light, preceding the blast wave. In fact, some fires started by the initial heat of a nuclear explosion might be blown out by the following blast wave and winds. Thermal radiation burns people directly and also in-directly by igniting their clothes or surroundings. People within two miles of the nuclear explosions at Hiroshima and Nagasaki got first-degree burns on their exposed skin; some were burned through their clothing, particularly if they wore dark colors, which absorb thermal radiation.

In both cities, thermal radiation started many fires, and others were ignited as a result of broken fuel lines and electrical short circuits. The damage was greatest in Hiroshima, where flat terrain and concentration of wooden buildings helped produce

The charred remains of a young Japanese boy in Nagasaki, about a half mile from ground zero.

---

groups of raging fires. The result was not a true fire storm, however, as is commonly reported in accounts of the Hiroshima catastrophe. Fire storms as a result of bombing occurred in Hamburg and Dresden, Germany, and in Tokyo. They produced much greater heat and burned so rapidly that people died in the streets and in shelters from heat alone or from carbon monoxide. According to the best available evidence, such deaths did not occur at Hiroshima, though there is reason to believe that nuclear explosions can cause true fire storms.

The flames went unchecked because most fire stations were destroyed and 80 percent of the firemen were killed or injured. Units from neighboring districts could do little because roads were blocked by collapsed buildings and water pipes were melted or broken. In all, both blast and fire reduced about eight square miles of Hiroshima to ashes. At Nagasaki there was less fire, and the force of the bomb was confined somewhat by surrounding hills; the greatest damage was limited to about four square miles.

In addition to great heat and blast, the first nuclear weapons produced something not found in ordinary explosives: radiation in the form of gamma rays, neutrons, and alpha and beta particles (or rays). Alpha and beta particles travel relatively short distances, so they never reached the ground beneath the aerial bursts over Hiroshima and Nagasaki. Neutrons and gamma rays are more powerful and reached the ground, buildings, plants, and people in an area with a radius of about a mile. All of these forms of radiation are strong enough to change the electrical charge of an atom, transforming it into an ion, and are called ionizing radiation. This powerful energy can destroy or damage cells in humans and other living things.

There is still some uncertainty about the makeup of the initial burst of radiation at Hiroshima and Nagasaki. Gamma radiation near ground zero was undoubtedly strong enough to kill anyone who might have somehow survived the blast and heat. But the effects of radiation may last long after a nuclear weapon explodes. Neutrons from the explosion collide with soil, building materials, and other matter. Most of the material that absorbs neutrons becomes radioactive and continues to emit radiation for some time. Several days after the attack on Hiroshima and Nagasaki, this sort of radioactivity was detected hundreds of yards from ground zero. It further endangered survivors and also rescue workers from outside areas.

Some soil, rock, and other debris were vaporized by the fireball and sucked up into the mushroom-shaped clouds that towered over Hiroshima and Nagasaki. This matter later condensed into particles containing radioactive nuclei from the fission process. The return of these contaminated particles to the earth's surface is called fallout. The amount of fallout at Hiroshima and Nagasaki was quite small since the bombs exploded in the air, not on the ground. At Hiroshima some fallout descended as "black rain," an explosion-generated rainstorm

Near ground zero no buildings were left standing in Nagasaki.

that killed fish in a river, contaminated the water of a reservoir, and made people ill. In 1981, thirty-six years after the explosions, radioactivity levels almost thirty times higher than average for Japan were found in soil near Nagasaki's Nishiyama reservoir.

In general, the heaviest fallout pieces—some as large as coins—settle out quickly, while the lightest may stay in the atmosphere for years and are carried great distances. Fallout particles can cause serious burns if they touch skin, or other harm if inhaled or swallowed with food. The radiation they emit damages cells, causing cancers and other abnormalities.

Since 1945 a joint United States-Japan research effort has been aimed at determining the radiation exposure of Japanese people at varying distances from ground zero. This is a difficult task because shielding by buildings has to be taken into account. Also, vital information about the radiation released by the two bombs was a classified secret for many years. Not until 1965 were tentative dose estimates completed for all victims. Then, in 1976 a government estimate of the radioactive output of the

Hiroshima bomb was finally released. This report led to further research and revision of the estimated doses that Japanese people experienced.

The unit used to measure radiation dosage is the rem, which stands for *r*oentgen *e*quivalent in *m*an. It represents the amount of radiation needed to produce a particular amount of damage to living tissue. (For some kinds of ionizing radiation, including gamma rays, a rem is equal to another unit of radiation dosage, the rad.) The total dose of rems determines how much harm a person suffers. At Hiroshima and Nagasaki, people received a dose of rems at the instant of the explosions, then more from their surroundings and, in limited areas, from fallout. Their experience is our single greatest source of information about the effects of gamma rays on humans.

Although a dose of just 25 rems causes some detectable changes in blood, doses to near 100 rems usually have no immediate harmful effects. Doses above 100 rems cause the first signs of radiation sickness: nausea, vomiting, headache, and some loss of white blood cells. Doses of 300 rems or more cause temporary hair loss, but also more significant internal harm, including damage to nerve cells and the cells that line the digestive tract. Severe loss of white blood cells, which are the body's main defense against infection, makes radiation victims highly vulnerable to disease. Radiation also reduces production of blood platelets, which aid blood clotting, so victims of radiation sickness are also vulnerable to hemorrhaging.

Half of all people exposed to 450 rems die, and doses of 800 rems or more are always fatal. Besides the symptoms mentioned above, these people suffer from fever and diarrhea. There is no effective treatment; death occurs within two to fourteen days.

These generalizations are based on thousands of individual cases at Hiroshima and Nagasaki. For example, a fourteen-year-old boy was admitted to a Hiroshima hospital two days after the explosion, suffering from a high fever and nausea. Nine days later his hair began to fall out. His supply of white blood cells dropped lower and lower. On the seventeenth day he began to bleed from his nose, and on the twenty-first day he died.

His case illustrates an important fact about radiation sickness. The boy had probably received a dose of 450 rems or more, yet his symptoms were about the same as those of a person who received about 300 rems. Medical science has no way of telling the difference between people who have received fatal doses and will die despite all efforts and others who received less radiation and can be saved. (Treatment includes blood transfusions and bone-marrow transplants.)

At Hiroshima and Nagasaki, the few surviving doctors observed symptoms of radiation sickness for the first time. In his book *Nagasaki 1945*, Doctor Tatsuichiro Akizuki wrote of the puzzling, unknown disease, of symptoms that "suddenly appeared in certain patients with no apparent injuries."

Several days after the bombs exploded, doctors learned that they were treating the effects of radiation exposure. "We were now able to label our unknown adversary 'atomic disease' or 'radioactive contamination' among other names. But they were only labels: we knew nothing about its cause or cure . . . . Within seven to ten days after the A-bomb explosion, people began to die in swift succession. They died of the burns that covered their bodies and of acute atomic disease. Innumerable people who had been burnt turned a mulberry color, like worms, and died . . . . The disease," wrote Dr. Akizuki, "destroyed them little by little. As a doctor, I was forced to face the slow and certain deaths of my patients."

Doctors and nurses had no idea of how their own bodies had been affected by radioactivity. Dr. Akizuki wrote, "All of us suffered from diarrhea and a discharge of blood from the

There is no way to distinguish people who have received fatal doses of radiation from those who received less radiation and can be saved by medical treatment.

gums, but we kept this to ourselves. Each of us thought: to-morrow it might be me . . . . We became stricken with fear of the future."

Dr. Akizuki survived, as did several hundred thousand others in or near Hiroshima and Nagasaki. (At least ten people who had fled from Hiroshima to Nagasaki survived *both* bombs.) In time the nuclear war survivors were given a special name: *hibakusha* ("explosion-affected persons"). They have suffered physically, from cataracts, leukemia and other cancers, mal-formed offspring, and premature aging, and also emotionally, from social discrimination.

Within a few months of the nuclear explosions, leukemia (cancer of the blood) began to appear among the survivors at an abnormally high rate. Some leukemia victims were fetuses within their mothers' wombs when exposed to radiation. One child who was born two days after the Hiroshima explosion eventually died of acute leukemia at the age of eighteen. The number of leukemia cases has declined with time, but the incidence of lung cancer, thyroid cancer, breast cancer, and cancers of other organs has increased among the hibakusha.

Each new death attributed to the effects of the nuclear explosion at Hiroshima is recorded in that city's Peace Memorial Museum. The museum also exhibits photographs and drawings, a lump of melted roof tiles fused with human bones, and other grim mementos of the world's first nuclear war.

"In the case of nuclear weapons, the American public has been totally and deliberately excluded from policy decisions which are vital for its very survival."—*Kosta Tsipis*

# 3

# The Arms Race

In the years just after World War II the United States built several hundred nuclear weapons and did its best to keep the process secret. Its monopoly ended sooner than expected, however. In late August 1949 high levels of radioactivity were detected in an air sample collected over Long Island, New York. Airborne radioactive dust was then tracked back to the North Pacific, and analysis of the samples left no doubt about the source: a nuclear explosion in Central Asia, within the Soviet Union.

Tensions increased between the two superpowers. The behavior of the United States and the Soviet Union has been likened to that of insecure, competitive children—one built a bomb, then the other built a bomb, so the first decided to make an even bigger bomb. It was the hydrogen bomb, sometimes called the H-bomb or the super. The H-bomb, however, was not something hastily dreamed up in response to the Soviet's first nuclear bomb test. It had been considered a possibility since the 1920s and discussed by the physicists who worked on the Manhattan Project's fission bombs.

Fission involves the breakup of the nuclei of atoms of such heavy elements as uranium and plutonium. Fusion is the joining together of nuclei of lightweight atoms, usually forms or isotopes of hydrogen. Pound for pound, fusion produces three times more energy than fission. More importantly, it does not depend on a chain reaction. Fission bombs are rather wasteful, since their explosion ends a chain reaction before it uses up all of the available fissionable material.

Scientists calculated that a fusion bomb could be a thousand times more powerful than the fission weapons then developed. The United States already had plans for an improved fission bomb as powerful as 500,000 tons of TNT (500 kilotons). Producing a mightier fusion weapon was opposed by many top American physicists. Nine of them, including Enrico Fermi and J. Robert Oppenheimer, scientific director of the Manhattan Project, made up the General Advisory Committee of the Atomic Energy Commission. In October 1949 they recommended strongly that we not make an all-out effort on the H-bomb, on the basis of economic, military, and ethical considerations.

It would be an enormously costly project that might not work out, they argued. Militarily, the United States already had

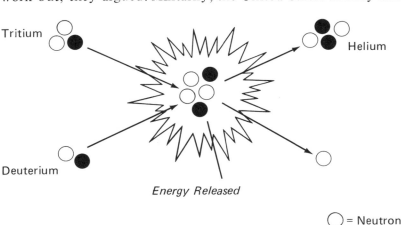

**NUCLEAR FUSION REACTION**

a large stock of fission weapons—more than enough to destroy the Soviet Union even if the Russians developed and used the H-bomb. The scientists also concluded:

"We base our recommendations on our belief that the extreme dangers to mankind inherent in the proposal wholly outweigh any military advantage that could come from this development. Let it be clearly realized that this is a super weapon; it is in a totally different category from an atomic bomb. The reason for developing such super bombs would be to have the capacity to devastate a vast area with a single bomb. Its use would involve a decision to slaughter a vast number of civilians. We are alarmed as to the possible global effects of the radio-activity generated by the explosion of a few super bombs of conceivable magnitude. If super bombs will work at all, there is no inherent limit in the destructive power that may be attained with them. Therefore a super bomb might become a weapon of genocide."

Nevertheless, in early 1950 President Truman ordered research to proceed on H-bomb development. Within days of his decision came news that a spy had for years passed secret information about U. S. nuclear weapons to the Soviet Union. This revelation fueled American fears of the Russians and hastened the effort to bring the H-bomb to test stage.

A race for the first super bomb was on. Both the Americans and the Soviets exploded preliminary devices in the early 1950s; then on March 1, 1954, the United States tested its first true H-bomb at Bikini Atoll in the Marshall Islands. An explosion equal to 8 million tons of TNT had been predicted; the actual yield was nearly 15 million tons. Human inventiveness and fear had produced a weapon whose destructive power was measured not in kilotons but in megatons (millions of tons of TNT). This initial H-bomb is the largest ever tested by the United States. The biggest Soviet bomb, tested in 1961, yielded nearly 60 megatons.

The cloud of the July 25, 1946 Bikini H-bomb envelops old warships anchored to measure radiation and blast effects.

Aside from destroying most aquatic life within a 200-square mile area in the Pacific Ocean, the first Bikini H-bomb provided Americans with a dramatic lesson about radioactive fallout. It was much greater than expected, covering an area of 7,000 square miles, and a last-minute wind shift carried radioactive particles to a small Japanese fishing vessel 90 miles away. All twenty-three crewmen fell ill with radiation sickness, and one died from liver damage. Inhabitants of Rongelap Atoll, about 150 miles from the explosion, suffered burns from beta rays and also swallowed radioactive iodine in their food and water. They were evacuated two days after the test. Nearly all of the Rongelap children underwent surgery to remove abnormal growths from their thyroid glands; several women were later afflicted with thyroid cancer. The Rongelap people were allowed to return to their atoll after three years, but twenty years later other atolls in the region were still too radioactive to visit safely. Soils on Bikini Atoll contained such high levels of cesium-137 that human settlement there would be dangerous until late in the next century.

The dangers of radioactive fallout became more apparent as further bomb tests were conducted by the United States, the Soviet Union, Great Britain, and other nations that had attained nuclear capability. In 1962 alone, the two superpowers tested more than a hundred nuclear devices. An agreement to end aboveground tests was finally worked out in 1963 and was signed by more than a hundred nations. France and China continued to test nuclear weapons in the atmosphere, while the other nuclear powers conducted underground tests. India, the sixth nation to join the "nuclear club," produced a 12-kiloton explosion underground in 1974, claiming it was a device to be used for peaceful purposes such as excavation projects.

---

Rongelap mothers bathing their children. Nearly all of the children required thyroid gland operations as a result of their exposure to fallout from the Bikini H-bomb.

One 1962 test revealed an effect of nuclear explosions that had been overlooked by the United States. A rocket carried an H-bomb 248 miles above the Pacific, where it exploded. An instant later, lights went out in the Hawaiian Islands, 800 miles away. Fuses blew and burglar alarms went off. These electrical disruptions were caused when x-rays and gamma rays from the explosion struck air molecules, releasing electrons. The electrons spun around and down the lines of the earth's magnetic field, producing a tremendous burst of electromagnetic energy. This electromagnetic pulse (EMP) traveled swiftly to the earth's surface, where it was collected by wires and antennas and caused damage to electrical circuits.

Since the test-ban treaty prevented further high-altitude bursts, scientists have had to study the effects of EMP in other ways. It is now recognized as a potentially great problem in nuclear war, capable of disrupting electrical power and communications and thereby also crippling a nation's ability to wage war or to recover from it.

The end of atmospheric tests did not stop refinement of nuclear arms. The earliest bombs, whether fission or fusion, were cumbersome, heavy devices. Only one or two could be carried by a large aircraft, and the first generation of H-bombs had yields of 10 to 15 megatons. They made little sense because few cities or other targets required 10 megatons for their destruction. In his book *Weapons and Hope*, physicist Freeman Dyson wrote, "There is not much satisfaction, even for the most bloodthirsty general, in using ten megatons to wipe out an airfield or a city when a tenth of a megaton would do the job just as well."

Modern nuclear warheads may weigh as little as 100 pounds, can be fired in 8-inch artillery shells, and yield as little as a tenth of a kiloton. Warheads on long-range missiles have yields from one tenth of a megaton to 20 megatons (on some models of Soviet SS-18 missiles). A tenth of a megaton sounds like a small weapon, but keep in mind that it is seven times more powerful than the Hiroshima bomb.

Regardless of their explosive power, most modern warheads are called thermonuclear weapons. The Greek word *thermé* means heat, and great heat is needed to cause the nuclei of lightweight atoms to fuse. Each weapon is triggered by chemical explosions that cause a small plutonium bomb to fission. Energy and neutrons from fission then strike the fusion warhead, which consists of solid lithium deuteride. When a neutron strikes a lithium deuteride nucleus, helium, tritium, and deuterium are produced. Compressed inward, the core of deuterium and tritium reaches a temperature of 20,000,000° F. Fusion occurs and the bomb explodes. Most thermonuclear weapons also have an outer shell of uranium-238 around their core, and the uranium atoms fission when struck by neutrons from the fusion process. Thus, in order, a fission reaction, a fusion reaction, and then another fission reaction occur within less than a millionth of a second as a thermonuclear warhead explodes. About half of the yield of a thermonuclear weapon comes from fission and half from fusion.

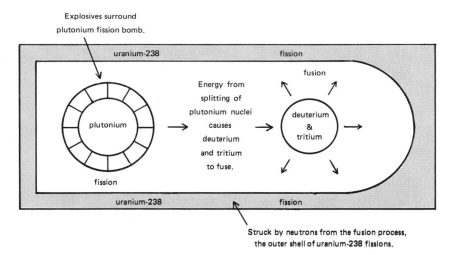

**A THERMONUCLEAR WEAPON**

The arsenal of the United States includes some fission bombs and also some neutron bombs. The latter are small thermonuclear weapons designed to produce less blast and more neutron radiation than usual. They are sometimes called enhanced radiation warheads. The increased radiation is produced by omitting the uranium shell around the deuterium-tritium core. When the fusion reaction occurs, neutrons are not absorbed by uranium but radiate outward from the exploding bomb. High-speed neutrons can penetrate concrete and thick metal armor. A 1-kiloton neutron bomb exploded in the air can deliver a fatal dose of neutrons to everyone within a radius of half a mile and cause radiation sickness in everyone within a mile. Its blast would destroy most structures within a mile. These effects are not greatly different from other thermonuclear weapons of equal strength.

Refinements of nuclear weapons have been accompanied by improved ways of getting them to targets. Early fission bombs were so big that, aside from sneaking one into a port city by ship, the only practicable delivery method was large aircraft. The United States built hundreds of long-range bombers capable of carrying nuclear warheads and also perfected ways to refuel them in flight from tanker planes. Soviet bombers had less range and lacked in-air refueling capability.

Americans had little reason to fear a Soviet air attack until 1957. In that year a powerful Soviet missile carried the first man-made satellite, *Sputnik*, into space, and the Soviets also tested an intercontinental missile. The vast reaches of the Atlantic and Pacific oceans no longer protected the United States, whose cities were now in range of Soviet land-based missiles.

These are ballistic missiles, which lack wings or winglike surfaces. They are thrust into the stratosphere by the power of one or more rockets, each with a fuel supply and an engine or engines. When the fuel of the first stage is used up, that part of

Soviet strategic nuclear weapons are predominately large land-based intercontinental ballistic missiles.

the missile drops off, and the next stage takes over. The last stage is the unpowered warhead, which is equipped with a heat shield for protection as it plunges through the atmosphere at 20,000 miles per hour to its target. It can arrive at its target within half an hour of being launched.

The United States began developing such long-range missiles in 1954. Its program was speeded up in response to the 1957 Soviet successes, and by 1962 the United States had nearly 300 intercontinental ballistic missiles (ICBMs), while the Soviets had no more than 85. Since then the nuclear arsenals and the delivery systems of both nations have greatly increased and have also become more diverse and complex.

All nuclear weapons can be divided into two categories: strategic and tactical. Strategic weapons, like ICBMs, are intended for targets within the territory of another nation. Tactical weapons, such as short-range missiles and nuclear artillery shells, are already deployed for war on foreign soil or at sea. In reality, tactical weapons can also be used for strategic missions.

In the early 1980s, the United States had about 9,300 strategic nuclear warheads. In terms of their destructive power, 40 percent was carried by long-range aircraft, a little less than 40 percent by ICBMs, and the remainder by submarine-launched ballistic missiles (SLBMs). In terms of actual numbers of warheads, however, submarines carried roughly half, because each missile was loaded with multiple weapons.

Until 1968, all missiles were capable of carrying just one nuclear warhead. Then the United States tested MIRV—the Multiple, Independently targetable, Reentry Vehicle—a missile with two or more warheads, each of which can be guided to a separate target.

The front end of a MIRV missile is called the bus. It is covered by a metal cone or shroud that drops away as the bus coasts through space. The bus consists of several warheads (the reentry vehicles or RV of MIRV) attached to a structure, called the postboost vehicle, which contains a guidance system and small rockets. The guidance system directs the firing of the rockets, which steer and turn the bus until it is in a preprogrammed position. A warhead is then released so that it will enter the atmosphere on a path toward its target. The bus then maneuvers to a new position and releases another warhead "passenger," and so on until the bus is empty.

American Poseidon and Trident missiles, launched from submarines, can carry from 8 to 14 MIRV warheads. The huge Soviet SS-18 missiles, 11 feet in diameter and 120 feet long, have been tested with 10 but can carry an estimated 30 MIRV weapons. United States MIRV systems have been quite accurate in tests and are being made more so. Also, radio signals sent from a ground or air command center to the MIRV bus can re-aim warheads to new targets.

In addition to its 9,300 strategic nuclear weapons, the United States in the early 1980s had about 15,000 tactical warheads deployed in Europe, Asia, and elsewhere, including on its Atlantic and Pacific fleets. These weapons included nuclear artillery shells, land mines, and antisubmarine mines and missiles. The Soviet Union was estimated to have about 7,000 similar tactical warheads concentrated in its west and in eastern Europe (the Warsaw Pact nations). In strategic weapons, most of the Soviet's 7,300 warheads were in long-range missiles. Soviet ICBMs carry nearly 80 percent of the nation's destructive power and of its strategic warheads. Submarine-launched missiles carry 15 percent and long-range bombers the remaining 5 percent.

The nuclear arms race continues. Each decade brings new developments and refinements in weapons and their delivery systems. After decades of carrying bombs and short-range missiles, American long-range bombers can now be loaded with up to 20 cruise missiles. Each 20-foot-long missile can carry a 200-kiloton warhead. Launched from the airplane in flight, a cruise missile looks like a flying torpedo with tiny wings. It is a pilotless airplane, powered by a lightweight engine, that flies at about 450 miles an hour toward a target up to 1,500 miles away. It can skim along close to the ground, avoiding detection by radar. Cruise missiles can also be launched from the ground, from ships, or from submarines.

An important trend in the arms race is toward greater missile accuracy. Early ballistic missiles were not very accurate—the American Atlas ICBM, for instance, could not reliably hit within 5 miles of its target. Missile accuracy is measured in terms of "circular error probable" (CEP), which refers to the radius of a circle around a target within which half of all missiles fired at the target would land. The U.S. Titan II, an ICBM that can carry a 9-megaton warhead 15,000 miles, has a CEP of 1,430 yards, or eight-tenths of a mile. In other words, half of all Titan IIs reaching their targets would strike that close or closer to them.

The most advanced American guidance system used in Minuteman III ICBMs gives warheads a 50 percent chance of hitting within less than 1,000 feet of their targets. The MX missile, a new ICBM under development in the United States, may have a CEP of less than 300 feet for each of its ten 300-kiloton warheads.

The more accurate a missile, the more threatening it is, especially to the underground concrete cylinders called silos in which ICBMs are kept and from which they would be launched in war. Silos are built to withstand great overpressure, but highly accurate missiles can probably be "silo-busters." Thus, increased accuracy of both American and Soviet missiles stimulated further efforts in the arms race.

A cutaway drawing of an underground silo for a Minuteman III missile.

The nuclear arsenals of the United States and the U.S.S.R. are large, complex, diverse, and ever changing. To them can be added about a thousand warheads of the other four known nuclear powers. (The nuclear club may also include Israel and South Africa, while Iraq, Libya, and Pakistan are among several nations considered likely to develop their own nuclear weapons in the near future.)

The trend has been toward smaller, "smarter" weapons, so the fears of enormous H-bombs expressed in 1949 by prominent physicists were unfounded on that point. Otherwise, their warnings of possible mass slaughter of civilians, of alarming global effects of radioactivity, and of genocide were prophetic. The combined world arsenal, as of 1984, was about 50,000 nuclear weapons. Together, they total a million times the destructive power of the bomb that devastated Hiroshima and "provide" nearly three tons of TNT for every person on earth.

# 4

# One Megaton, One City

Television, newspapers, and other media bring us news of "little" wars between and within nations, of debates over defense budgets, of controversies over the need for new weapons, and of progress, or the lack of it, in arms-limitation negotiations. Until the late 1970s, the subject of what an actual modern nuclear war might be like was largely ignored by the public. Now hypothetical nuclear attacks have been described in several authoritative studies, and the possibility of nuclear war has become more real and personal and much harder for people to ignore.

What would happen if the Soviet Union and the United States actually used some of their extraordinary stocks of nuclear warheads? Until this happens we cannot truly know. There are so many unknowns, including physical, biological, and behavioral factors, which would influence the outcome. Is a limited war possible, or would any use of a nuclear weapon lead inevitably to the unleashing of thousands of others? Would there be some warning, some time for partial evacuation of cities? And what about the time of the day, the prevailing winds, the season—all of which affect the location of people, their exposure to heat, blast, radiation, and fallout, and their chances of survival afterward.

A surprise attack on a clear summer day, for example, would cause maximum burn casualties. Many people would be outdoors, unprotected from thermal radiation, which is unimpeded under clear conditions. If visibility was only 2 miles, the heat from a 1-megaton warhead would cause second-degree burns up to 2.7 miles from ground zero. In much clearer conditions—visibility 10 miles—people up to 6 miles from ground zero would receive such burns.

Taking such factors into account, in 1979 the United States Office of Technology Assessment (OTA) published a report, *The Effects of Nuclear War*. It assessed the effects of an attack on a single city and also other hypothetical uses of nuclear weapons in war. The OTA researchers assumed that a large city—Detroit, Michigan—was attacked without warning at night, when most of the 4.3 million residents of that metropolitan area would be at home.

The season and time of day affect people's clothing and shelter— and thus their exposure to a nuclear explosion.

According to the OTA scenario, a 1-megaton warhead explodes downtown, near the Detroit Civic Center, ripping a crater 200 feet deep and 1,000 feet across. The blast creates an overpressure of 12 pounds per square inch within 1.7 miles of ground zero. Only the strongest reinforced concrete walls remain standing within this circle, and all 70,000 people estimated to be in that area die. Many of them melt, burst into flames, or char. (In a daytime attack, with people at work and school, 130,000 more people would die in this zone.)

The next mile outward, between 1.7 and 2.7 miles from ground zero, is blasted with an overpressure of about 5 pounds per square inch. Skeletons of some buildings remain, but their outer walls are blown out. Automobiles are destroyed by the blast or by collapsing buildings. Streets are filled with debris, especially where the taller buildings once stood. Two miles or more from ground zero, people receive radiation of about 50 rems or less—not a lethal dose. However, of the 250,000 people within the 1.7- to 2.7-mile ring, half are killed, and most of the rest are injured by fire, by collapsing buildings, and by being hurled against objects by 150-mile-per-hour winds.

In the next concentric ring, between 2.7 and 4.7 miles from ground zero, an overpressure of 2 pounds per square inch and accompanying winds are still strong enough to destroy or damage most homes and to crack walls and frames of larger buildings. Industrial plants are badly damaged; most aircraft and hangars at the Detroit City Airport are destroyed. Only about 20,000 of the 400,000 people in this zone are injured. Many of the injuries are burns from extensive fires that rage unchecked for more than 24 hours. Fires start and spread more readily in the partly damaged buildings of this area than in the collapsed structures closer to ground zero.

In the outermost band of damage, 4.7 to 7.4 miles from ground zero, an overpressure of 1 pound per square inch damages

The blast effects on an unreinforced brick house are shown by these before-and-after photos. The house was located nearly a mile from ground zero of a 1955 nuclear test explosion.

homes moderately and stronger structures lightly. Most of the 600,000 people in this region survive, although one out of four is injured.

The surface blast tosses many tons of radioactive debris into the air, and within a few minutes fallout from the stem of the huge mushroom cloud begins to descend on the remains of Detroit. Survivors who emerge from shelter to help others or to flee are exposed to several hundred rems of radioactivity in the first hour. Most of them die. About an hour after the explosion, radioactive particles begin to fall to earth from the mushroom cloud itself. Some areas in Detroit and within 30 miles of the city receive deadly 3,000 rems from fallout.

---

An airburst 1-megaton weapon creates a greater area of pressure damage and more burns and fires than a groundburst weapon, but yields no significant fallout.

0    2    4    6    8    10
Miles

The path of the fallout depends on wind direction and the terrain. A northwest wind, for example, would carry the fallout southeast, across Lake Erie to Cleveland and Akron, Ohio, and to Pittsburgh, Pennsylvania, 200 miles away. Assuming a steady 15-mile-per-hour wind, in a week's time the cumulative radiation dose would be 900 rems in Cleveland, 300 in Akron, and 90 in Pittsburgh. Given enough warning, several million people would evacuate as quickly as possible from the fallout's probable path. (A wind from the southwest would bring fallout to sparsely populated areas of Ontario, Canada.)

The dawn after the nuclear explosion would reveal large parts of Detroit in flames, a quarter of a million people dead, half a million injured. Since debris would block most streets, many of the injured would go without treatment for days. Thousands would die before help reached them. Seventy percent of Detroit's hospitals would have been destroyed or seriously damaged; just 5,000 beds therefore would be available in lightly damaged or unharmed hospitals.

A few thousand hospital beds for half a million injured people! Moreover, many thousands would suffer from serious burns, and no injury puts more of a demand on hospital services. Frequent changes of burn dressings are needed to control infection, and up to fifty surgical operations may be required. Hundreds of the Detroit victims would be children, who are affected more severely than adults by burns. For eight-year-olds burned over 60 percent of their bodies, the survival rate in hospitals is only 20 percent, but it increases to 50 percent for those treated in burn-care centers. Fewer than a hundred of the 6,000 general hospitals in the United States have such centers. At most, fewer than 2,000 severely burned patients could be treated at any one time in the entire nation. In Detroit, thousands of people, burned over 20 to 90 percent of their bodies, would go without treatment for days. Many would die in unimaginable agony.

A burn victim in Nagasaki. Nuclear explosions cause many burns, and serious burns require intensive medical care.

Rescue efforts would be severely hampered by blocked streets, high levels of radiation, and lack of water and electricity. Crews would have to wear protective clothing against radioactivity, and the total exposure of each worker would have to be limited to avoid hazardous doses of radiation. Eastern areas of the metropolitan region, which are the zone of maximum fallout, would be dangerously radioactive. Two weeks would have to pass before it would be safe to enter these areas and begin rescue and cleanup efforts. The city airport lies within this "hot" zone. Fortunately, two other airports were not affected by the blast or fallout. Rescue workers and equipment would pour in, and the injured would be airlifted to hospitals all over the nation.

Telephone, electricity, and other services would be gradually restored to the periphery of the city. In time, Detroit could be rebuilt, but a large area near ground zero would remain a rubble-strewn wasteland; ten years would pass before radiation dropped to safe levels there. Even the outer regions, up to seven miles from ground zero, probably wouldn't be safe for permanent residents until three years passed.

According to the OTA study, if the same 1-megaton warhead exploded 6,000 feet above Detroit, there would be no crater and virtually no fallout. Pressure damage would extend farther outward, however. The result: over a million casualties, including half a million dead within the first hour.

A 1-megaton warhead has 80 times the explosive power of the Hiroshima bomb, but both the Soviet Union and the United States have more powerful weapons. What if a warhead of 25 megatons exploded in the air over Detroit or a similar city?

At Hiroshima, some buildings remained standing about a third of a mile from ground zero of the airburst 13-kiloton weapon. A 1-megaton weapon is eighty times more powerful.

Actually, larger weapons distribute their destructive power less efficiently than smaller ones, so damage would not be 25 times greater. According to the OTA report, blast damage reaches outward 30 miles, destroying virtually all buildings, bridges, and other structures in the entire metropolitan area. Nearly 2 million people die immediately, and about 1.4 million are injured. No hospitals exist; all rescue workers, medical supplies, and other aid has to come from outside the Detroit area. All survivors must be evacuated and resettled elsewhere. It is questionable whether the Detroit wasteland will ever be rebuilt.

To some extent, the OTA's grim scenario can be applied to any city, keeping in mind that each locality has distinctive features that may influence the effects of a nuclear explosion. Nagasaki's hills, for example, muted the impact of the 22-kiloton bomb that exploded there. Also, the OTA researchers, comparing Detroit with Leningrad in the Soviet Union, found that Detroit has many wooden, single-family homes, while most Leningrad residents live in ten- to twelve-story apartment houses made with steel frames and concrete walls. Thermal radiation would ignite fewer fires in Leningrad than in Detroit. However, the population of the Soviet city is much more concentrated, so a 1-megaton airburst would cause twice as many deaths and injuries as in Detroit.

In the United States, the Arms Control and Disarmament Agency has calculated the casualties that would be caused by nuclear attack for every city with a population of 25,000 or more. Whatever your locality, you can look it up and read the grim statistics of the devastation that would be caused by several different warheads, from 50 kilotons to 20 megatons. Do you live in or near San Francisco? According to the agency's 1979 report *Urban Population Vulnerability in the United States*, a 1-megaton airburst over San Francisco would kill 624,000 people and seriously injure 306,000.

These figures for San Francisco and the agency's estimates for other cities are seriously underestimated, in the opinion of Dr. H. Jack Geiger, a professor of community medicine and Director of the Program in Health, Medicine, and Society at City College of New York. All estimates are based on the notion that everyone would be at home. Dr. Geiger believes this is unrealistic. If the Soviet Union attacked population centers rather than military or industrial targets, the attack would most likely be timed to occur when maximum numbers of people are away from their homes, on a weekday during work and school hours.

The agency's calculations also do not include possible deaths or injuries from fire storms, yet conditions for such infernos exist in many cities. Taking these two factors into account, Dr. Geiger believes that it is conservative to increase casualties by 25 percent—to 780,000 dead and 382,500 injured in the case of a 1-megaton airburst over San Francisco.

In his 1981 essay "Illusion of Survival," Dr. Geiger described some injuries that would afflict the survivors: "Hundreds of thousands of 'survivors' would suffer crushing injuries, simple and compound fractures, penetrating wounds of the skull, thorax and abdomen, and multiple lacerations with extensive hemorrhage, primarily in consequence of blast pressures and the collapse of buildings. (Many of these victims, of course, would also have serious burns.) A moderate number would have ruptured internal organs, particularly the lungs, from blast pressures . . . . Superimposed on these problems would be tens of thousands of cases of acute radiation injury, superficial burns produced by beta and low-energy gamma rays, and damage due to radio-nucleides in specific organs. Many would die even if the most sophisticated and heroic therapy were available; others, with similar symptoms but less actual exposure, could be saved by skilled and complex treatment. In practical terms, however,

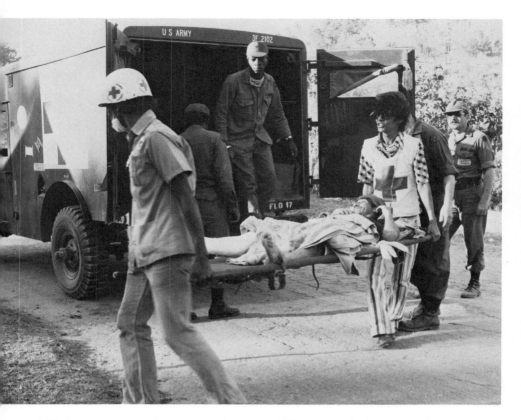

U.S. Army rescue workers carry a victim of a 1976 earthquake in Guatemala. We expect such aid when disaster strikes, but in a nuclear war, stricken areas may not get much help from outside.

there will be no way to distinguish the lethally-irradiated from the non-lethally-irradiated."

Along with burns, these are the short-term medical problems. But who will treat these people? Agreeing with the OTA assessment of conditions after an attack on Detroit, Dr. Geiger wrote, "Physicians' offices and hospitals tend to be concentrated in central-city areas closest to ground zero. If anything, physicians will be killed and seriously injured at rates greater than those of the general population, and hospitals similarly have greater probabilities of destruction or severe damage. Of the approximately 4,000 physicians in San Francisco County, perhaps half would survive a one-megaton airburst; of the 4,647 hospital beds in the county, only a handful would remain."

Surviving doctors will vary, of course, in their training and their willingness to treat the injured. And medical care will be given without x-rays, blood transfusions, drugs, and other supplies and equipment, unless assistance comes from outside the shattered city. Most likely, many people will die without treatment or with inadequate treatment.

These studies of the horrifying effects of a single nuclear warhead are sobering and important to know about, but in one way are profoundly unrealistic. They remind us of every other disaster that has befallen humankind. We all know what happens when an earthquake, hurricane, flood, or other such tragedy strikes. News of the disaster goes out, and people respond. Rescue workers, medical teams, food, blankets, and other needed materials pour in. To some extent the same thing occurred in the first nuclear war, as the rest of the Japanese nation helped rebuild Hiroshima and Nagasaki.

Today, in the event of a nuclear attack on a city, rescue workers would wisely avoid high levels of radioactivity, but we would still expect an extraordinary rescue and rebuilding effort. This has been our experience—*but modern nuclear war is beyond our experience.* If it happens, few imagine that just two cities, say Detroit and Leningrad, will be attacked. More likely, hundreds or thousands of targets, including many cities, will be struck. The devastation described in the OTA study for Detroit might strike all large cities in the United States. (Studies of such large-scale assaults are described in later chapters.)

Our notions of massive assistance must be discarded. There might well be no significant help from outside a stricken city. Electricity, fuel supplies, and water might be cut off indefinitely. No food would come in, nor would desperately needed medical supplies and assistance. Without treatment, even those with minor injuries might face death because exposure to radiation reduced their resistance to infection. Futhermore, survivors would be undernourished and crowded together in the housing that remained standing. Infection and death would be all around; in fact, there would be many thousands of unburied human corpses, as well as the remains of dead pets, livestock, and other animals.

Conditions would be ripe for the spread of such communicable diseases as food poisoning, influenza, typhoid fever, and hepatitis. Even such diseases as tuberculosis and plague, now of low incidence in the United States, could cause much sickness and death under the conditions that would probably exist after a nuclear attack.

Most physicians believe that nuclear war is the greatest threat to health that society has ever faced. In 1981, at the first congress of the International Physicians for the Prevention of Nuclear War, the participants concluded: "The earth would be seared; the skies would be heavy with lethal concentrations of radioactive particles, and no response to medical needs should be expected from medicine."

"The soldier died in Hiroshima. Men, women, and children alike now will inhabit the nuclear battlefield. Every citizen is now a soldier, every home has become a target."—*Bernard Lown*

# Limited Nuclear War

An intercontinental ballistic missile takes about thirty minutes to travel between the United States and the Soviet Union. Missiles launched from submarines would need as little as eight minutes to reach targets in either nation. The exhaust plumes of missile launches can be detected by infrared sensors on warning satellites, which in a few seconds process and transmit data to command centers below. That leaves a few minutes for a nation under attack to respond—to rule out a false alert by means of radar images of the missiles, to assess the attack, and then to initiate retaliation. Detection of an unmistakable salvo of several hundred incoming missiles would almost certainly stimulate a massive onslaught in return, before a single missile had struck.

These short response times make a limited nuclear war seem unlikely, particularly in the case of a surprise attack, but military strategists envision situations in which war might be limited—to parts of Europe, or to purely military targets, or to oil refineries, for instance. In 1983, physicists Frank von Hippel and Barbara Levi and military analyst William Arkin published their study of a hypothetical nuclear war in East and West Germany. They were particularly interested in the effects on civilians of nuclear attacks aimed only at military targets. They chose the two Germanies because the two most powerful military forces ever assembled in peacetime confront each other across the border between East and West Germany. The most likely invasion corridors of a European war lie in the Germanies. Should war break out in Europe, the Germanies would be quickly involved; should nuclear arms be used, they would probably explode first in East and West Germany and be used there most intensely.

The analysts believed that the first use of nuclear weapons in Europe would be an act of desperation, "an attempt either to reduce the strength of an apparently imminent nuclear attack by the other side or to prevent a major defeat or irreversible loss of territory in a war being fought with non-nuclear weapons."

Forces of the Warsaw Pact and of the North Atlantic Treaty Organization (NATO) have warheads and delivery systems grouped at about 135 known sites in the Germanies. As a crisis grew or as war began, either or both sides would try to move these weapons in order to make them less vulnerable to attack or capture. The act of moving them itself might be misinterpreted by the enemy and trigger a nuclear attack.

In addition to the weapons themselves, other targets of military importance include command and communication centers, missile sites, naval bases, air bases, troop concentrations, bridges, and fuel and munition storage areas. There are more than a thousand such targets in East and West Germany. For the purposes of this study, the researchers assumed that 171 of the air bases, missile bases, and nuclear weapon storage sites would be targets of nuclear-tipped missiles or bombs. (Eighty-six of the targets are in West Germany, 85 in East Germany.)

Pershing missiles with nuclear warheads are among the weapons deployed by NATO forces in West Germany.

Such an attack would use only a small fraction of the warheads that could be delivered to targets in the Germanies by aircraft or by short- to medium-range missiles. The power of the available weapons ranges from 1 kiloton to more than 1,000 kilotons. The largest yield—1,100 kilotons—is contained in warheads carried by NATO bombers and fighter-bombers. Soviet SS-20 missiles carry three 150-kiloton warheads, and British submarines, under NATO control, carry Polaris missiles, each with three 200-kiloton warheads. For the purposes of this study, the analysts assumed that each of the warheads used would yield 200 kilotons, about ten times the power of the Nagasaki bomb.

Whether warheads exploded on the surface or in the air would be a significant factor. Low-altitude bursts would effectively destroy aircraft and missile sites without producing much fallout. A surface burst, however, would rip a huge crater in an airfield and also leave the area highly radioactive. In a real war, some NATO military strategists believe that certain vital military targets would be struck by both surface-burst and airburst warheads.

The researchers assumed that people would have some warning and that most would seek shelter in basements, with only 5 percent of the basements reinforced against nuclear attack. Even so, a 200-kiloton airburst would kill 40,000 people in an area of average population, and about 500,000 in an average urban area. A surface burst would kill less initially, but fallout would cause additional deaths downwind. Because of prevailing winds, fallout casualties would be greatest in East Germany and in Poland.

Many of the most important military targets in the two Germanies are in densely settled areas. Therefore, the study concluded, the nuclear exchange would kill between 1.6 million and 10.6 million people, depending on where the weapons exploded. Airbursts would kill between 1.6 and 4.2 million, ground bursts between 4.7 and 8.3 million, and a combination of both would kill between 5 and 10.6 million people. Total casualties could excede 20 million people.

The same research team also considered the effect on civilians of a conventional war in the Germanies that escalates to the use of nuclear battlefield weapons. NATO and Warsaw Pact forces have thousands of such arms, including short-range missiles, land mines, artillery shells, and bombs. Their explosive yield ranges from one-tenth of a kiloton to 100 kilotons. One-kiloton neutron (enhanced radiation) warheads were picked as a middle-yield weapon by the analysts.

Radiation from such weapons would kill everyone—immediately or over a span of a few weeks—within 2 square miles of ground zero. Both attackers and defenders tend to use towns and cities as protective cover, so many civilians would be at risk. Even if the target was a column of tanks, many civilians would be killed or injured because the Germanies are densely populated. Using average population density, the researchers calculated that a thousand civilians would die as a result of each nuclear explosion; use of a thousand battlefield warheads would kill a million civilians.

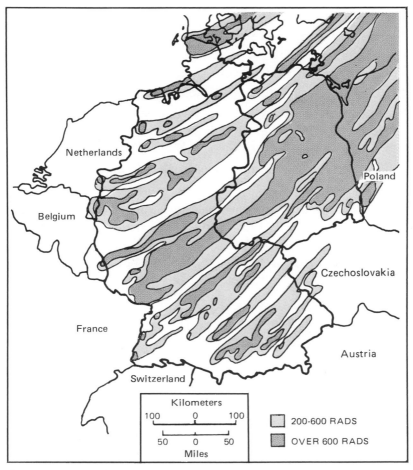

Typical June winds would produce this fallout pattern in the Germanies and eastward into Poland.

The study concluded: "Unfortunately, while the catastrophic consequences of a deliberate attempt to destroy Eastern or Western Europe with nuclear weapons are generally understood, both sides are now prepared to use nuclear weapons against 'purely military' targets, if it is necessary to avoid defeat in a major conflict. Europe, however, is densely populated; the intermixing of military and civilians is intimate; and the areas of death which would be caused by the use of even 'small' battlefield nuclear weapons are very large . . . . Even the purely military use of nuclear weapons on any scale large enough to achieve militarily significant results would result in . . . mass slaughter of civilians."

The authors of the study had calculated the *least* damage a limited nuclear war might cause to the population of one area of Europe. They also expressed skepticism that any nuclear exchange would actually be confined to the Germanies: "By the time warheads were used against large fractions of significant classes of military targets . . . it is likely that the exchange of nuclear blows would be building up with such great rapidity that all-out nuclear war would be inevitable."

Even though a limited nuclear war is unlikely to remain so, the studies of such hypothetical wars are useful because their effects are more imaginable than those of all-out nuclear war. Such studies make it possible to assess the damage wrought by an attack on separate categories of targets, including economic ones. In *The Effects of Nuclear War,* the Office of Technology Assessment (OTA) investigated the effects of a Soviet attack, using just ten SS-18 ICBMs, limited to U.S. oil refineries.

These are MIRV missiles, each carrying eight 1-megaton warheads. The area in which a MIRV missile can deliver its busload of warheads is called its footprint. Each load of warheads would be aimed at targets within a footprint of roughly 125,000 square miles, and there would be one such footprint for each of the ten missiles. This is no handicap

for the attack, since many oil refineries in the United States
are clustered together. (The map below shows the ten footprints
and the major cities located within these target areas.)

In this scenario, the attack strikes the 77 largest U.S.
refineries, and the three remaining warheads are used as second
weapons on very large targets. Each warhead explodes over its
target, at an altitude that allows the biggest possible area to be
struck by an overpressure of 5 pounds per square inch or more—
a circle with a radius of 4.3 miles from ground zero. (In a real
war, such accuracy and reliability would not occur, but many
more missiles would probably be launched to compensate
for malfunctions.)

In this hypothetical attack, ten Soviet missiles strike U.S. oil refineries with
multiple warheads. Each footprint on this map is struck by eight warheads.

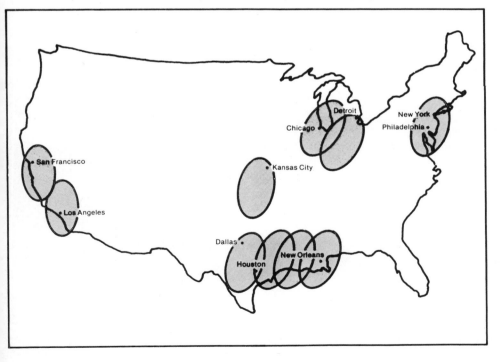

According to the OTA scenario, 64 percent of U.S. petroleum refining capacity is destroyed. Also wrecked or damaged are petroleum storage tanks, pipelines, petrochemical plants, rail lines, highways, and ports. Fires rage out of control for days, fueled by oil, gasoline, and chemicals; some may become fire storms, spreading destruction far beyond the blast zone, killing people directly or causing them to suffocate by sucking oxygen out of their shelters. Even without fire storms, more than 5 million people die immediately from the 80 airburst warheads. (This estimate may be conservative—it assumes that 10 percent of all people in large cities fled before the attack and that all of the rest are in basement shelters or inside single-family homes.)

Many thousands of these deaths occur in Chicago, Houston, Los Angeles, and other large cities near major refineries. The

An oil storage tank ablaze in Texas. Nuclear explosions at oil refineries have the potential of creating massive fire storms.

OTA researchers chose Philadelphia for detailed study of the effects of this oil-refinery attack. Two large refineries are located south of the city's center, on the Schuylkill River. According to the OTA scenario, a 1-megaton warhead explodes in the air over each refinery, and 410,000 people die instantly within 5 miles of the twin bursts. Eight large hospitals lie within about 2 miles of the refineries; another nine hospitals are located between 2 and 3 miles away. Little is left of these facilities or their staffs.

All stored oil is either destroyed immediately or burns in fires that rage out of control. Three of four electric power plants are damaged or destroyed, but so is much of the industry and downtown business district that once needed electricity. The Philadelphia International Airport is heavily damaged, as are major highways and rail lines within a few miles of the explosions. Other severely damaged structures include a U.S. naval shipyard, City Hall, and the University of Pennsylvania.

All of this destruction and death is a side effect of what some war strategists might call a precise "surgical" strike against two oil refineries. It is plain to see that, just as there are no purely military targets for nuclear weapons, there are also no purely economic targets.

After the 80 warheads struck the United States, the behavior of people would depend greatly on whether they believed another attack was likely. Chaos would reign if they felt more missiles might be on the way. Once they felt safe, efforts toward recovery could begin, but years would be needed to restore the nation's oil-refining capacity, due in large part to the death of many people who are skilled in building and operating refineries. The United States would have to survive on a third of its former refining capacity and on even less of its oil-port facilities. The government would allocate petroleum products to certain vital users, including military forces, police, firefighters, and railroads.

In the aftermath of a nuclear attack on petroleum refineries, every activity dependent on gasoline and oil would be halted or severely cut back.

According to the OTA report, "The demise of the petroleum industry would shatter the American economy, as the attack intended. A huge number of jobs depend on refined petroleum: manufacture, sales, repair, and insurance of cars, trucks, buses, aircraft, and ships; industries that make materials used in vehicle manufacture, such as steel, glass, rubber, aluminum, and plastics; highway construction; much of the vacation industry; petrochemicals; heating oil; some electric power generation; airlines and some railroads; agriculture; and so on. Thus, many workers would be thrown out of work, and many industries would be forced to close."

Use of private cars would be severely reduced, and businesses that depend heavily on their use would suffer greatly. Besides those already mentioned, these include all stores in shopping malls, fast-food restaurants, and suburban real estate and home construction. The economic blows would reach Japan and other automobile-exporting nations too. Many businesses would go bankrupt. Some would prosper, however. Bicycles and other vehicles that use little or no gasoline would be in great demand, as would buses and other mass-transit carriers.

The OTA report states: "Patterns of industrial production would shift dramatically because of these changes, forcing massive shifts in demand for skills and resources. Many people and factories would be oriented to the production of things no longer in demand; it would take many years for the economy to adjust to the sudden, massive changes imposed by the attack."

The health-care resources of the United States would be overwhelmed by the millions of injured and would be stretched thin for years. The overall quality of health care would decline. Actually, some effects of reduced petroleum supplies would be beneficial as people ate less meat (which requires large amounts of energy to produce) and exercised more by walking to work. These small advantages would come slowly, however, while the onslaught of great problems would be swift. It is clear that warheads from just 10 missiles could throw the United States into severe difficulties for many years.

The United States is fully capable of inflicting similar damage on the Soviet Union. Soviet petroleum refineries are fewer in number but more widely dispersed. In a hypothetical attack described by the OTA, the Soviet targets are 24 refineries and 34 petroleum storage areas, with multiple warheads aimed at some of the larger targets. Seven Poseidon missiles, launched from submarines, carry a total of sixty-four 40-kiloton warheads, and three Minuteman IIIs carry a total of nine 170-kiloton warheads. The attack destroys 73 percent of Soviet refining capacity and 16 percent of its oil storage.

Exploding in the air above the targets, the warheads kill 836,000 people instantly. This estimate is based on the assumption that everyone lives in multistory steel and concrete

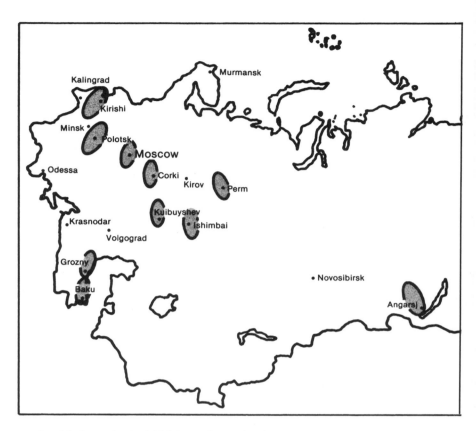

In this hypothetical U.S. attack on the Soviet Union, ten MIRV missiles deliver warheads to the footprint areas on the map, where Soviet oil refineries are concentrated.

buildings; deaths would nearly double if all dwellings were single-family homes. Even the highest estimated death toll is much less than in the hypothetical attack on the United States, because Soviet refineries are located farther from large cities than those in the United States. Also, the average yield of American warheads is less than that of the Soviets. Since the goal of this attack is to deal an economic blow, not to kill people, the relatively low-yield American weapons are quite effective.

Soviet life would be sharply disrupted. Until it became clear that the war was over, millions of reservists would be mobilized, and the military would have first claim on fuel stocks. When the threat of war lessened, much of the reduced petroleum production would be shifted to agriculture. Soviet agriculture normally uses a third of the nation's gasoline and diesel fuel, and its crop yields are barely adequate even in peacetime. Food production would present the greatest challenge to the Soviets. Wherever possible, human labor would be substituted for farm machinery. Large-scale malnutrition and even starvation might well occur.

According to the OTA study, the Soviet standard of living would drop from austere to grim, but the changes in people's lives might not be as shocking as those in the United States, where today's citizens have a higher standard of living and have never experienced war on their homeland, as many living Russians have.

Students of nuclear war believe that the most likely targets of a limited attack would not be economic but military—an opponent's strategic military weapons. This is called a counterforce attack. The goal: to destroy so many of the enemy's long-range missiles and bombers that it can retaliate only weakly or not at all.

To disarm, not destroy, is, in fact, the announced nuclear strategy of the Soviet Union. A Soviet counterforce attack on the United States has been studied by several government agencies, including the OTA and the Department of Defense (DOD), and by consultants to the Senate Committee on Foreign Relations and to Congress's Joint Committee on Defense Production. A report from the latter, titled *Economic and Social Effects of Nuclear War on the United States*, was prepared by Dr. Arthur M. Katz, an expert on matters of science and public policy, who in 1982 published an expanded and updated version, *Life After Nuclear War.*

In his scenario, adapted from the DOD study, the Soviet Union simultaneously attacks 1,054 ICBM silos, 54 Strategic Air Command (SAC) air bases, and 2 nuclear submarine bases. Each missile launching site is hit with two 1-megaton ground bursts, each SAC base with a pattern of three 1-megaton airbursts (designed to catch some bombers soon after takeoff), and each submarine base with a 1-megaton ground burst.

At first the DOD study had proposed that airbursts would be used against all targets, but ground bursts were later thought to be more likely. American ICBM silos are estimated to be able to withstand overpressures up to 2,000 pounds per square inch. To destroy the silos and their missiles, a half-megaton warhead would have to burst within 1,000 feet. Also, a warhead that is designed to detonate upon impact is more reliable than one that is set to explode at a certain height above its target. Furthermore, the electronic trigger device of a warhead that is

About 40 percent of U.S. strategic warheads are carried by long-range B-52Hs, which are stationed at Strategic Air Command bases.

supposed to explode in the air can be disrupted by a nuclear explosion; the airburst of one warhead can disable other incoming warheads. This is called fratricide. Ground bursts are thought to be a reliable way to avoid or reduce fratricide and to ensure a high level of target destruction.

The Soviet counterforce attack destroys more than half of the U.S. ICBMs in their silos and inflicts heavy damage to SAC and submarine bases. Bursts at ICBM silos cause relatively little immediate harm to civilians, but many SAC and submarine bases are near cities, including Charleston, South Carolina; Little Rock, Arkansas; and Sacramento, California. Overall, more than 16 million people would die within 30 days, and between 10 and 20 million others would be injured.

What remains of the nation's medical-care system is overwhelmed. Dr. Katz described another complicating factor that might affect medical care: "If the postattack period is an unstable and threatening military stalemate, which it is quite likely to be, the full utilization of the medical facilities and personnel of prime urban targets (large cities) will be diminished if not totally eliminated because of unplanned or planned evacuation. This situation could further degrade effective medical care for weeks or months."

More than a thousand ground bursts would produce great amounts of radioactive fallout. The map on page 71 shows how the prevailing winds of winter would influence fallout patterns. (Typical December-January winds are light compared to those of March. Strong winds can produce three times the deaths and casualties from fallout as weak winds.) Distribution of fallout is also affected by precipitation. Raindrops wash radioactive particles from the air, creating regions of intense radioactivity while reducing the amount that settles elsewhere.

Vast areas of the United States and also some parts of Canada would lie in the path of fallout. Radiation levels would rise sharply downwind a few hundred miles from each explosion. The 2.5 million residents of the St. Louis metropolitan area would have only an hour or so to protect themselves. Fallout from the Whiteman Air Force Base, 160 miles to the west, would bring radiation levels to about 3,000 rems in the first 24 hours. Some regions would have more time, perhaps several days, to prepare shelters or to evacuate, although, given the uncertainties of weather forecasting, people might not want to stake their lives on the predicted locations of fallout-free zones.

Most people would seek shelter. The OTA report *The Effects of Nuclear War* described some of the practical difficulties these people would face after a counterforce attack: "The time to seek shelter could be very limited (and people would not know how long they had), and people would want to get their families together. A shelter must have a sufficient protection factor. Fallout particles must be kept out of the shelter, which requires a ventilation system more complicated than an open window or door, and if anybody enters a shelter after fallout has fallen there must be some means of decontaminating the new arrival. Water is necessary; heat may be necessary depending on the time of year; sanitation is a problem. Finally, people could not tell how long it was necessary to stay in the shelter without radiation meters.

"The few hours after the attack would see a frantic effort to seek shelter on the part of most of the American population. Then, in densities and locations determined by the attack parameters and the weather, the fallout would descend. Many Americans would be lucky enough to be in areas where the fallout level was low. Many others . . . would be caught without shelter, or with inadequate shelter, and would die. Still others would suffer from a degree of radiation that would make them sick, or at least lower their life expectancy, but not kill

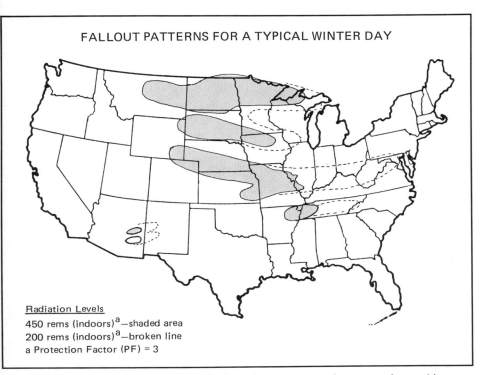

**FALLOUT PATTERNS FOR A TYPICAL WINTER DAY**

Radiation Levels
450 rems (indoors)[a]—shaded area
200 rems (indoors)[a]—broken line
a Protection Factor (PF) = 3

Given relatively light winter winds, a Soviet counterforce attack would produce these fallout patterns. Stronger winds would spread radioactive fallout even farther.

them. The trials of living in fallout shelters would be intensified by the fact that many people would not know which category they and their families were in."

In most fallout areas, radioactivity would reach reasonably safe levels within two weeks, though it would still be high by peacetime standards. Only then would populations in those regions begin to help the injured or evacuees, get back to work, and face the staggering economic and food supply problems. According to the research of Dr. Katz, about a third of U.S. manufacturing capacity lies within the fallout patterns of either a winter or March wind condition of a counterforce attack. Loss of a key industry, such as steelmaking, would affect many other businesses, and the disruption might last for several months or longer.

The American banking and financial systems would be thrown into turmoil, with many bankruptcies and defaults on loans and mortgage payments. For long periods, people would be unable to get their money from banks located in regions contaminated by fallout or actually destroyed by nuclear warheads. Also, insurance normally does not protect homes and businesses against the catastrophe of nuclear war. The main burden of repairing and rebuilding would probably fall on individuals and businesses, since the resources of state and federal governments would be overwhelmed. The U.S. government might have difficulty borrowing money or trading for goods abroad. In such an unstable time it might well be considered a poor credit risk by other nations, including those that normally supply a large share of U.S. petroleum needs.

The ICBM silos of the United States are located in the heart of its grain- and livestock-producing regions. Whatever the season, a Soviet ground-burst counterforce attack will bring heavy fallout contamination to large parts of the major U.S. food-producing states. Many farmers and other people in farm communities will be exposed to doses of 450 rems or more. Tens of thousands of these skilled individuals will die or recover slowly. Immediate crop losses will result. An attack just before or during harvest time would be especially costly, since work would stop and whole crops would go to waste. Radiation itself would be most damaging to young crop plants in late spring or early summer.

Radiation will also kill livestock. More than 40 percent of all cattle are raised in the states that will be contaminated by fallout. Meat supplies will drop sharply, prices will rise sharply, and many years will pass before the livestock supply returns to former levels. The entire food production and distribution system will be disrupted by deaths, injuries, fallout contamination, evacuation, economic chaos, and fear of radiation and new attacks. Even if crops are harvested in one area, there may be great difficulties in getting them processed and transported to the people who need them.

Since a counterforce attack is limited to military targets and kills "only" 16 million people immediately, more than 200 million will be alive and hungry. The United States government may find itself in a terrible bind, needing most of its reduced agricultural production at home, yet also deperately needing to sell grain abroad to earn precious income. Drastic cuts in grain exports will have great social and financial effects on other nations.

The Midwest, home of ICBM silos, is also the nation's main grain-growing region. Warheads aimed at missiles will also cripple U.S. food production.

In *Life After Nuclear War*, Dr. Katz points out that North America, and especially the United States, has become the breadbasket of the world: "The United States has exported 70 percent of its wheat, 20 percent of its corn, 20 percent of its oats, 15 percent of its barley, 25 percent of its sorghum, and 40 percent of its soybean production . . . . Thus, even if limited to a few years, a dramatic disruption in U.S. food production capacity leading to a significant restriction on the ability or desire to export could have serious and perhaps long-term worldwide repercussions on the international financial structure . . . world food supplies and prices, and even the distribution of world or regional power."

Dr. Katz also speculated about some of the psychological and social effects of a counterforce attack. In the short term, unless news of the damage and casualties was censored, many millions of people in all regions would be desperate to lessen their feelings of vulnerability. They would seek to get away from urban areas or other likely targets. Instead of a return to homes and jobs, there might be a massive exodus. Rural areas and small cities would be invaded by evacuees, and authorities would be challenged to provide enough food, shelter, and medical supplies. Such an invasion could lead to conflict between evacuees and residents and among people already under great stress.

In the long term, the actual survivors of blast and fallout, like the hibakusha in Japan, might become "living symbols of the society's vulnerability and impotence," particularly those millions of people who bore burn scars or other physical reminders of the nuclear attack. Just like those from Hiroshima, wrote Dr. Katz, they "might find themselves isolated, rejected, and denied adequate assistance—a basis for further conflict."

In its assessment of a Soviet counterforce attack, the OTA called the psychological impact an "imponderable."

The report simply said, "The United States has never suffered the loss of millions of people, and it is unlikely that the survivors will simply take it in stride. The suffering experienced by the South in the decade after 1860 provides the nearest analogy, and a case can be made that these effects took a century to wear off."

Even with all of these horrible effects, a Soviet counterforce strike like the one described would fail to achieve its goal: to destroy the ability of the United States to retaliate. Many ICBMs and SAC bombers would survive, and each of the three legs of the U.S. strategic triad is designed so that it alone could destroy the Soviet Union. More than 15 missile-carrying submarines are always at sea with a total of 2,500 MIRV warheads on board. In these weapons alone, the United States has the capability of inflicting an equal counterforce strike or much greater devastation on the U.S.S.R.

"Those observers who speak of 'recovery' after a holocaust or of 'winning' a nuclear war are dreaming. They are living in a past that has been swept away forever by nuclear arms."
—*Jonathan Schell*

# 6

# Large-Scale War

In the opinion of many military strategists, a counterforce strike aimed only at ICBM silos, air bases, and submarine bases is unrealistic. Any such attack would also include other facilities vital for waging war, especially the people and equipment involved in command, control, communication, and intelligence— called $C^3I$. These are among the most important targets in any war, since they make it possible for defenders to gather and process information, to make strategy, and to convey and change orders. For the United States the $C^3I$ targets include the president and other national leaders in Washington, D.C., the headquarters of the Strategic Air Command and of North American Air Defense, telephone switching centers, and communication and observation satellites.

A successful assault on the $C^3I$ of any nation would cripple its ability to fight back. It would also greatly increase the casualties of a counterforce strike, since some $C^3I$ targets are in cities. No doubt $C^3I$ facilities would be among the primary targets in an all-out war between the two superpowers. In 1982, a U.S. Department of Defense document set forth a war strategy based on decapitation ("to cut off the head"), meaning strikes at Soviet leadership and communication lines.

Either nation would probably use EMP (the electromagnetic pulse described in Chapter 3) in its assault on the $C^3I$ of the other. Four or five 1-megaton warheads from submarine-launched missiles, exploded 300 miles above the continental United States, would blanket the county, as well as much of Canada, Mexico, and Central America, with EMP. Actually, a single burst over the nation's center would probably be sufficient to damage most of its communication systems.

---

Within seven minutes of being launched, missiles launched from submarines could carry warheads over the center of the United States or the Soviet Union. Their high-altitude explosions would blanket either nation with the disruptive electromagnetic pulse.

Electrical and electronic equipment, as well as long-line communication systems and electric power grids, would be disrupted or destroyed. Writing in the January 1984 issue of *Scientific American*, foreign policy analyst John Steinbruner concluded, "It is not known exactly what would happen if the entire U.S. were to be subjected to the equivalent of thousands or perhaps tens of thousands of simultaneous, highly accelerated bolts of lightning, but any practical assessment must anticipate massive failures of communication systems, power supplies and electronic equipment."

Special equipment, such as surge arresters and bypass devices, offer protection from EMP, and the United States is taking steps to "harden" its military communications; Soviet systems are thought to be already more protected. Nevertheless, the strategic command systems of both countries are vulnerable to some extent, and this weakness is far more important than that of weapons. Thus, most military strategists assume that an all-out attack would begin with high-altitude bursts to produce EMP, followed by missiles aimed to destroy other elements of the opponent's $C^3I$ capabilities.

One comprehensive study of a massive Soviet attack was completed in 1970 by the Stanford Research Institute for the U.S. Office of Civil Defense. The investigators were asked to determine the smallest number of warheads that would wreck the U.S. economy to a point beyond recovery. They estimated that heavy damage would have to be inflicted on 34 basic industries, including drugs, chemicals, agricultural chemicals, petroleum refining, steelworks, metalworking machines, construction equipment, communications equipment, and engines and turbines. Near-total devastation of these and other basic industries could be achieved by attacking the 71 largest metropolitan areas with 500 one-megaton warheads and also by striking specific targets for 8 of the 34 key industries with 200 to 300 smaller one-kiloton warheads. Assaults on about 50 additional metropolitan areas, as well as small cities and some rural targets, would be needed to accomplish this goal. (In this hypothetical attack, all warheads are airburst, so fallout is not great.)

Of the 34 basic industries, the 8 most vital were judged to be petroleum refining; ironworks and steelworks; primary smelting and refining of zinc, copper, lead, and aluminum; engines and turbines; electrical distribution products; drugs; office machines; and mechanical measuring devices. Their destruction would cause severe shortages of vital materials and equipment and would practically halt all industrial activity.

Since the U.S. population is highly concentrated in certain areas, vast regions of the country would escape direct attack. A few states, including Idaho, Montana, Nevada, New Hampshire, and Vermont, would not be struck according to this scenario. But this mostly rural or semirural land would not support the surviving urban population or sustain any large-scale recovery.

Economically, most of the difficulties described for more limited wars would occur, but to a much greater extent. The entire nation's economic system would be in chaos, with many key workers dead, injured, or evacuated and with records inaccessible or destroyed. Devaluation of the U.S. dollar would have grim national and international effects; foreign trade with the United States would virtually cease.

More than half of all Americans live in the 71 largest metropolitan areas; nearly half of these people, between 70 and 90 million individuals, would be killed or injured. Since three-quarters of all doctors and other medical-care professionals would be casualties, many of the injured would probably receive no medical treatment, not even for relief of pain. Their survival rate would be low.

This catastrophe results from the use of between 700 and 800 warheads, only a fraction of the Soviet ICBM arsenal. In his book *Life After Nuclear War*, Arthur Katz compared this hypothetical attack to smaller strikes, including one using as few as 300 to 400 warheads. Even such a "little" attack, according to his research, would kill or injure between 20 and 30 percent of all Americans and destroy up to 35 percent of the nation's manufacturing capacity.

Heavy concentrations of population and industry in the United States makes this devastation possible; about 60 percent of its people live and work on just 1 percent of the nation's land. One-fifth live in the 150- by 550-mile area between Boston, Massachusetts, and Norfolk, Virginia. In the Soviet Union, population and industry are even more densely concentrated and therefore vulnerable to at least the same level of destruction. All studies agree that, no matter which side strikes first, mutual obliteration is the likely outcome. The ashes of communism and capitalism will be indistinguishable.

A satellite night photo records the lights of the eastern half of the United States, revealing heavy concentrations of population and industry.

The attack scenario prepared by the Stanford Research Institute and further developed by Arthur Katz is just one of many attempts to imagine such an event. A 1977 Department of Defense study estimated that between 155 and 165 million Americans would be killed by an attack of several thousand warheads if all were ground burst and no civil-defense measures were taken. If half of the warheads exploded high enough in the air to minimize fallout, the estimated fatalities would be 122 million. Analysts say that deaths would be further reduced if people had been evacuated from densely populated areas. Under such circumstances, according to the Defense Department study, fatalities would be 40 to 55 million. All estimates represent the number dead after 30 days; they do not account for the many injured people who would experience more lingering deaths.

In the 1950s, researchers set furniture and human dummies in houses close to aboveground nuclear bomb tests in Nevada.

In its report *The Effects of Nuclear War*, the OTA described the aftermath of a massive nuclear assault on the United States in which the damage inflicted on Detroit (described in Chapter 4) would fall upon thirty or more other cities with populations of a million or more. In these cities the OTA pictured: "Fires will be raging, water mains will be flooding, powerlines will be down, bridges will be gone, freeway overpasses will be collapsed, and debris will be everywhere. People will be buried under heavy debris and structures, and without proper equipment capable of lifting such loads, the injured cannot be reached

After an explosion, remains of the dummies are visible in the debris of a collapsed house.

and will not survive. The fortunate ones that rescuers can reach will then be faced with the unavailability of treatment facilities . . . . The entire area of holocaust will be further numbed by either the real or imagined danger of fallout. People will not know whether they should try to evacuate their damaged city, or attempt to seek shelter from fallout in local areas and hope there will be no new attacks."

When people believe the attack is over and when fallout drops to safe levels, communities that were spared will be overwhelmed by refugees. Many people will flee from the wreckage of their neighborhoods in blind hope that they will find safety somewhere else. Where? For many days after the attack no guidance will come from a shattered government or from radio or television, which EMP rendered inoperative in the first microsecond of the attack. People will decide on the basis of personal whim or rumors. Millions of them will be outdoors, trying to reach that elusive refuge, when the deadly fallout begins to settle upon them.

In the opinion of some analysts, the above description and earlier details of the aftermath of attack scenarios give an unnecessarily gloomy view of a nuclear attack on the United States. Some go so far as to say that people who dwell on the horrors of nuclear war are "masochistic deviates who enjoyed torturing themselves (and others) with images of pain and despair." Some confidently write how-to books on surviving nuclear warfare. And in the early 1980s, the Federal Emergency Management Agency (FEMA) advocated the view that "the United States could survive nuclear attack and go on to recovery within a relative few years," and proposed a civil-defense plan to ensure this.

Civil defense is controversial. Some people believe that such preparations against nuclear attack only encourage the idea that such warfare is reasonable. They feel that survival would not be a blessing—"the living would envy the dead." Others hold that people cherish being alive, that most would—in the long run—be glad that they survived nuclear war, and that adequate civil-defense measures can save many millions of lives.

The issue is made more complicated by an alleged "civil-defense gap" between the superpowers. The Soviet Union has, under miltary control, a program that involves building blast shelters for thousands of key personnel, planning for massive population relocation, and educating citizens about survival techniques, including the construction of fallout shelters. This program, according to the U.S. Central Intelligence Agency, could significantly reduce Soviet casualties in a nuclear war. A similar effort has been advocated for the United States.

There is much doubt, however, about the effectiveness of this Soviet program. Even if its people were removed from targeted cities, the masses of evacuees could later be spotted by observational satellites and targeted in their new locations. Also, a massive nuclear attack on the Soviet Union would ensure the death of many millions by starvation; shelters would just delay death, and evacuation would just change its location. Such avowed Soviet civil-defense goals as dispersing industries have not been achieved. Instead, Russian industry is highly concentrated and therefore highly vulnerable. The Kama River Truck Plant, for example, 600 miles east of Moscow, is the world's largest and combines six huge factories on 23 square miles of land. A single 10-megaton airburst warhead would lay it waste.

The Soviet people reportedly have little confidence in their government's plans. They note that the initial letters of the Russian words for the civil-defense program spell the word "coffin." And they joke:

First Comrade: "What does the government advise in case of nuclear attack?"

Second Comrade: "Wrap yourself in a shroud and walk slowly to the cemetery."

First Comrade: "Why should I walk slowly?"
Second Comrade: "So as not to cause panic."

In 1978, the responsibility of planning for American civil defense and for peacetime disaster emergencies was given to FEMA, and the actions of this agency have fueled the controversy over civil defense. According to a 1982 FEMA report, as much as 80 percent of the U.S. population could survive a nuclear attack of 6,559 megatons. Virtually ignoring fallout, FEMA emphasized that full-scale war would affect less than 5 percent of the nation's land. Therefore, given enough warning of an imminent attack, 150 million people could be relocated to safe rural "host" areas in three to five days. FEMA assumed that people would obey orders, travel in their own cars as well as in buses, and bring the items on a recommended list, including as much food as possible, bedding, clothes, first-aid kits, portable toilets, and hammers, saws, and other building tools. Evacuees would then join the host-area residents in preparing fallout shelters, both in existing buildings and outdoors. Meanwhile, according to FEMA, 4 million essential workers would not be part of this crisis relocation plan; they would willingly remain in the evacuated areas, on the job, with specially built blast shelters available for them.

The optimism of this proposal, which would cost an esti- mated $4.5 billion to set up, was shared by Thomas K. Jones, who in 1981 was appointed U.S. Deputy Undersecretary of Defense for Research and Engineering. He argued that nuclear war was not nearly so devastating as people had been led to believe. From Soviet civil-defense manuals he had learned how people can make simple fallout shelters by digging a hole in the ground, covering it with a couple of doors or some boards, then piling 3 feet of soil on top as protection against radiation. "It's the dirt that does it," he said. "If there are enough shovels to go around, everybody's going to make it."

Such optimism is unjustified in the view of many people familiar with the likely effects of a large nuclear attack. Radioactivity *can* be blocked by such obstacles as wood and soil, but an effective fallout shelter, as noted in the previous chapter, must be more than a hole in the ground covered with dirt. People must live in it, with sufficient food and water, for two weeks or longer. Air must flow in and out, but filters are needed to stop fallout particles from entering. Anyone in the shelter

A cutaway view of an underground shelter,
with vital ventilation equipment,
that is designed to protect people from
nuclear blast and fallout.

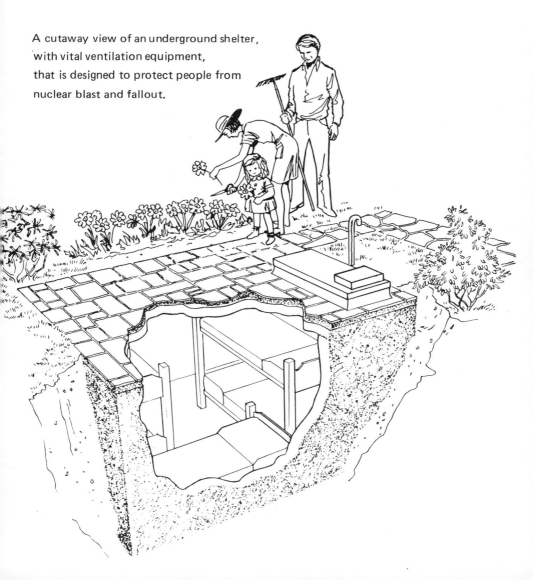

exposed to significant amounts of radiation may suffer from diarrhea and vomiting.

The OTA has pointed out: "Someone who vomited would not know if he had received a moderate, severe, or lethal dose of radiation; if he had severe psychological shock; if he had vomited because of contagion; or if he had some other illness. This uncertainty about one's own condition and that of one's loved ones, and nausea itself, would increase tension in the shelter."

Discomfort and stress would mark each passing hour as people waited for the reading on their dosimeter (assuming they had one) to tell them when outdoor radiation had fallen to levels low enough to permit them to emerge.

What kind of world would they find? According to a FEMA spokesman, life would be difficult, with a standard of living and technology like that of the 1930s or earlier. Yet the nation's resources would be harmed and depleted less than its population. Therefore, "in a sense, nuclear war could be expected to increase per capita wealth."

Following that logic, the fewer the survivors, the greater their wealth. More realistic, perhaps, is this description by Jonathan Schell in his book *The Fate of the Earth*: "Sitting among the debris of the Space Age, they would find that the pieces of a shattered modern economy around them—here an automobile, there a washing machine—were mismatched to their elemental needs . . . . They would not be worrying about rebuilding the automobile industry or the electronics industry; they would be worrying about how to find nonradioactive berries in the woods, or how to tell which trees had edible bark."

Some program aimed at civilian protection against nuclear attack may be wise, but many nuclear war experts believe that emphasis on evacuation and short-term biological survival is a cruel hoax on the public. Optimists speak of "recovery" after an attack, overlooking or ignoring the difficulties of restoring a modern technological economy. Arthur Katz has pointed out: "The factors that make rapid recovery from a small-scale disaster possible—limited damage, modest casualties, surviving leadership and technical skills, and the availability of external, easily mobilized human and material resources—will almost certainly be absent following a nuclear attack involving several hundred weapons targeted at a nation's industrial base."

People could exist for a time on undamaged stocks of food, fuels, drugs, critical equipment, and other goods and materials. Then, rather than restoring the smashed modern technological economy, survivors would struggle to create a new and more primitive one. "In effect," according to the OTA report, "the country would enter a race, with economic viability as the prize. The country would try to restore production to the point where consumption of stocks and the wearing out of surviving goods and tools was matched by new production. If this was achieved before stock ran out, then viability would be attained. Otherwise, consumption would necessarily sink to the level of new production and in so doing would probably depress production further, creating a downward spiral. At some point this spiral would stop, but by the time it did so, the United States might have returned to the economic equivalent of the Middle Ages."

In the study of possible nuclear wars, it is relatively easy to estimate the numbers of dead and injured, to gauge the reach of fallout, to describe physical damage. It is much harder to say how people will behave, yet the psychological, social, and political effects of nuclear war are of vital importance. They have been described to some extent in previous chapters.

How humans act during ordinary emergencies may not be relevant, except that they show a range of behavior. During an electrical blackout, a blizzard, or a flood, some people pitch in and help, while others loot homes and stores. However, no disaster so far experienced by humanity, not even Hiroshima and Nagasaki, is comparable to a large-scale nuclear attack and its aftermath.

People needing help will outnumber potential helpers, and even those who try to assist the injured will not have the skills or medicines necessary to treat the many people in need. Feelings of helplessness, failure, and guilt will predominate. Long after the war ends, massive numbers of the living will not be fully productive because of injuries or chronic illness and will remain an economic and emotional drain on others.

Stressful conditions will not ease for a long time, nor will feelings of apathy. In *Life After Nuclear War*, Arthur Katz observed, "Persons entering Hiroshima and Nagasaki after the attack found an apathetic and disorganized population. For months after the bombing, the Hiroshima survivors did not function effectively. It was the intervention of outsiders with resources and leadership that revitalized Hiroshima."

Some analysts warn that people may feel hostile and distrustful of the leadership that brought this catastrophe to their lives. Respect for authorities will drop if—or, more likely, *as*—they fail to effectively carry out relief and recovery programs. Survivors will be primarily concerned with personal safety and basic survival. Law and order may break down. (After the bomb exploded, Hiroshima became "infested with burglars.") Is it farfetched to imagine people fighting, even killing, over scarce medicines or food? The only viable government may be local, and the formerly united states might break into several competitive and hostile regional governments. A former superpower may resemble an underdeveloped nation.

A nation is more than its population and its leaders. All-out nuclear war would devastate the social structure of the United States by killing a large percentage of its business executives,

The devastating psychological blows of nuclear war may leave entire populations apathetic and disorganized.

scientists, educators, performers, and other highly skilled individuals. Many of the diverse institutions that make up our society, including professional sports teams, the television and film industry, and great libraries, museums, universities, and teaching hospitals, would be lost.

It is impossible to quantify these losses or to say with certainty that they will occur. But it is important to understand that a nuclear war can do more than smash buildings and radiate people. It can also crush the human spirit and tear a society apart.

"The vulnerability of the environment is the last word in the argument against the usefulness of shelters: there is no hole big enough to hide all of nature in."—*Jonathan Schell*

# 7

# Nuclear Winter

---

The most ambitious attempt to look in detail at a hypothetical large-scale nuclear war appeared in a special issue of *Ambio*, an international journal of the human environment, published by the Royal Swedish Academy of Sciences. In 1983 this study was published as a book entitled *The Aftermath: The Human and Ecological Consequences of Nuclear War.*

An *Ambio* advisory group described how and where nuclear explosions would occur, then asked thirteen experts, including physicians, physicists, radiation biologists, and economists (many from the United States) to analyze the possible effects from the perspective of their special knowledge. In the scenario, war breaks out at about 11 A.M. New York time, 6 P.M. Moscow time, on a weekday in early June 1985.

In one sense it cannot be called an all-out war. The problem, wrote the advisory group, "is to choose a set of targets for fifty to sixty thousand nuclear warheads. There is so much overkill in the arsenals that the exercise becomes overwhelming. It is impossible to find 'reasonable' targets for all of these. In our 'limited' scenario, we have only targeted 14,737 warheads, comprising less than half the megatonnages in the 1985 arsenals, or about 5,750 megatons."

In the *Ambio* study, the size of the warheads ranges from 100 kilotons to 10 megatons, with 90 percent in the 200–500 kiloton range. Most of the U.S. warheads strike the Soviet Union and Eastern Europe, while those of the Soviets are more widely dispersed, exploding in the United States, Canada, Western Europe, and China. This is a true world war, with warheads also striking South Africa, Australia, Cuba, and North and South Korea, although few are used in the Southern Hemisphere. Worldwide, 6,620 ground-burst warheads are used on military targets, 4,970 ground-burst warheads on population targets (1,514 cities with populations ranging from 100,000 to more than 10 million), and 3,136 airburst warheads on large industrial targets and such energy-related sites as oilfields and hydroelectric stations. Twenty-one warheads are also used to close key shipping straits, and some 300-kiloton weapons are water burst in attempts to destroy at-sea submarines.

To prepare maps showing patterns of early fallout, the advisory group used world weather patterns of a past June day. Fallout patterns drawn on the map showed those areas receiving at least 450 rads (or rems), sufficient to kill half of the people exposed. Each explosion was assumed to be unrelated to others, but in a real war some fallout patterns would overlap, producing even greater doses of radiation.

Of the urban population of nearly 1.3 billion in the Northern Hemisphere, about 750 million people would be killed outright and about 340 million seriously injured. Only about 200 million would be uninjured in the initial attack, though this may be an underestimate since explosion-caused fires were not taken into account. With most medical facilities destroyed, "the injured would have to fend for themselves, with whatever help might be available from untrained survivors."

Some of the injured and unharmed survivors would die in a second wave of illness caused by fallout radiation, and

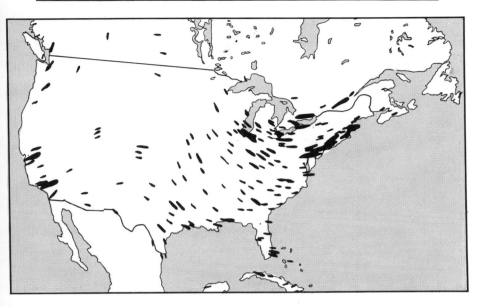

In the *Ambio* scenario of world nuclear war, the areas marked on this map of North America would receive at least 450 rads (or rems) of radiation—enough to kill half the number of people exposed.

still more from starvation and blood poisoning. Many would die from cholera and hepatitis (diseases caused by poor sanitation and contaminated water), other infectious diseases, and, eventually, from leukemia and other cancers caused by radiation. According to the analysis of two radiation biologists, the toll from radiation would be very high: survivors would suffer from 5.4 million to 12.8 million fatal cancers; 17 to 31 million people would be rendered sterile; and 6.4 to 16.3 million children would be born with genetic defects during the century following the nuclear world war.

The *Ambio* advisory group pointed out that the total of immediate and delayed deaths from radioactivity would be even higher if nuclear power plants were destroyed. An attacker might find reactors tempting strategic targets. Economically they represent a large capital investment and a source of electricity that is not easily replaced. Militarily, they represent a source of deadly radiation that could be loosed on a population and its homeland. In a sense, an attacker would get two bombs for the price of one by smashing a nuclear power plant with a warhead. If, for example, a 1-megaton warhead exploded at a 1,000-megawatt reactor, lethal radiation would be spread over more than 500 square miles—an area the size of Lake Erie—which is a third larger than that contaminated by the weapon alone.

The contents of a reactor are quite different from those of a thermonuclear weapon, which produces mostly short-lived radioactive isotopes that threaten life for several weeks or months. A reactor's fission products include such long-lived isotopes as strontium-90, cesium-137, and iodine-131. Blasted from a nuclear power plant and scattered over the land, this radiation would make large areas uninhabitable for decades, perhaps for more than a century. A warhead burst at a storage site for reactor wastes would strew even greater amounts of even more long-lived radioactivity, effectively rendering thousands of square miles inaccessible and useless to people for generations.

Although the *Ambio* scenario did not include reactors as targets, the advisory group warned: "In Western Europe, where many reactors are in operation and more are being built or planned, an attack on them would make practically the whole of these and neighboring countries uninhabitable by ordinary standards of radiation safety for years or decades. The same would be true for North America and Japan."

In the opinion of many strategists, however, nuclear reactors and waste-storage sites are unlikely to be attacked. Assuming that each opponent covets the land and resources of its adversary, it would avoid contaminating large areas with long-lived radio-activity. Nuclear weapons in the hands of a terrorist group or a fanatical political leader are seen as a greater threat to nuclear reactors.

In their analysis of the *Ambio* war scenario, experts on agriculture and economics envisioned conditions basically similar to those described in the previous chapter. Surviving urban dwellers would migrate to the country to forage for food and to plant new crops, but most of the harvesting and planting would be done by hand, not machine. The new harvests would be much smaller than in preattack times because of reduced acreage planted and shortages of fuel, fertilizers, and pesticides. Supplies might be sufficient in some areas simply because of the greatly reduced population—there would be many fewer mouths to feed. Food-importing nations would be almost completely cut off from their usual sources; in some cases the result could be catastrophic.

Plants vary greatly in their vulnerability to radiation. Forest trees are quite sensitive, and ecologist George Woodwell concluded: "The radiation exposures required to transform a forested zone into an impoverished landscape are well within the range of contemporary war, a few hundred to many thousands of roentgens. The areas affected might be large, tens to hundreds of square miles per bomb." Because of variations in weather and terrain, some areas would be spared while others received heavy doses. "The result," wrote Woodwell, "would probably be a mottled necrosis [death] of the landscape, with whole valleys escaping virtually untouched by fallout, others scorched by radiation and subsequently by fires feeding on the devastation."

In the opinion of French economist Yves Laulan, world nuclear war would take civilization back to the Dark Ages, with emphasis on basic necessities and "a return to the most elementary form of exchange used by primitive societies—the barter system." Destruction would be concentrated in the industrialized nations, and the more technically advanced the society, the greater the damage and the obstacles to recovery. Most of the developing or Third World countries—in Asia, Latin America, Africa, and the Middle East—would not be hit by missiles or bombs, but they depend heavily on the industrialized nations as sources of grains, fertilizers, and agricultural equipment, and as export markets for raw materials, including petroleum. Ruin of the rich industrial nations would bring increased starvation, illness, and political turmoil to the Third World. If such nations as India, Mexico, Brazil, Nigeria, and Indonesia were somehow able to keep their fragile industrial societies alive, they would become the new world powers, albeit at a comparatively humble level.

All-out nuclear war would end food exports from rich nations and leave poor nations with no outside aid against starvation.

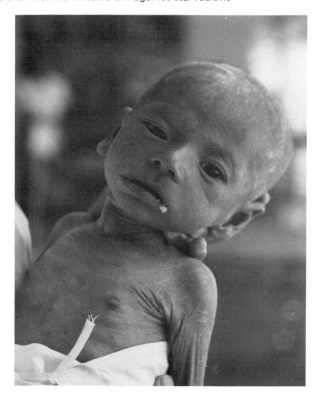

The *Ambio* study made clear that nuclear war would be an unprecedented catastrophe for everyone on earth, combatants and noncombatants alike. It also marked an important step forward in human attempts to understand the implications of nuclear arms.

The brief history of nuclear weapons development has given us several unpleasant surprises, including greater yield of radiation and more deaths than expected from the Hiroshima bomb, cancer-causing radioactive fallout from early weapons tests, and the disrupting effects of EMP on electrical and electronic equipment. This history has also been marked by warnings from different groups of scientists. Physicists, who released the nuclear genie from its bottle, were the first to alert the public—and presidents—to the awesome power of nuclear weapons and the folly of a nuclear arms race. Physicians have warned that medical science cannot give care to the casualties that would result from a nuclear war. And now biologists, ecologists, atmospheric chemists, and physicists have discovered another unforeseen effect of nuclear warfare and caution us that nuclear explosions might inflict grave damage on the global climate and thereby threaten all life on earth.

The environmental consequences of nuclear war were largely overlooked until the mid-1970s. In 1975, a committee of the National Academy of Sciences (NAS) released a report on *Long-Term Worldwide Effects of Multiple Nuclear-Weapons Detonations*. The committee found evidence that nitric oxides produced by bursts of many megatons and blown into the stratosphere would deplete the earth's ozone layer, which shields the earth's surface from excessive amounts of ultraviolet radiation from the sun. This could cause increased skin cancers, as well as harmful effects on climate and plant and animal life. The NAS study concluded, however, that if such changes occurred, they would last only a few years.

The 1979 OTA report on the effects of nuclear war reported on new developments that were related to the possible threat of ozone depletion. Further research had led atmospheric chemists to decide that harm to the ozone layer would be caused by bursts of very high-yield warheads exploded at altitudes of 80,000 feet or higher. Such use of high-yield weapons would make no tactical sense in a war, and since the trend in weaponry is away from high-yield warheads, serious depletion of the earth's ozone layer seems less likely than before.

Neither the NAS nor OTA report had much to say about other possible environmental effects of nuclear weapons. Then, in 1981, the *Ambio* advisory group asked scientists to look in detail at the possible effects of large-scale nuclear war on such resources as freshwater supplies, ocean ecosystems, forests, and the atmosphere. Research on atmospheric effects was a joint effort by John Birks, atmospheric chemist at the University of Colorado, and Paul Crutzen, meteorologist and atmospheric chemist at West Germany's Max Planck Institute for Chemistry.

They agreed that ozone depletion would probably not be a problem, but found other disturbing possibilities that had been previously overlooked. Large-scale nuclear war would ignite fires in many cities that would not be extinguished. Besides these fires, many natural oil and gas wells would also burn unchecked, as would fires in grain fields, grasslands, and forests. Vast woodlands grow close to many likely targets in the United States, Canada, and the Soviet Union, so many wildfires would start during and after the war.

Birks and Crutzen estimated that about 4 percent of forests in the Northern Hemisphere would burn, some for as long as two months. They were startled to calculate that as much as 400 million tons of thick smoke would rise from all fires. Great smoke plumes containing carbon dioxide, carbon monoxide, and dark particles of soot and ash would cloud the

Birks and Crutzen estimated that fires caused by large-scale nuclear war would send as much as 400 million tons of smoke into the lower atmosphere.

lower atmosphere of the northern half of the earth, blocking sunlight from its surface for several weeks.

This condition would reduce or even eliminate the possibility of growing agricultural crops over large areas of the Northern Hemisphere, also possibly killing most plankton, which are the foundation of ocean food chains. In addition, people and other living things near city and industrial fires would be enveloped in smog containing carbon monoxide, hydrogen sulfide, methane, hydrocarbons, ammonia, and other noxious gases.

Birks and Crutzen concluded: "It is also quite possible that severe, worldwide photochemical smog conditions would develop with high levels of tropospheric [lower atmosphere]

ozone that would likewise interfere with plant productivity . . . .
It is, therefore, difficult to see how much more than a small
fraction of the initial survivors of a nuclear war in the middle
and high latitude regions of the Northern Hemisphere could
escape famine and disease during the following year."

As Birks and Crutzen had hoped and urged, their pioneering
study for *Ambio* led to further investigation. By coincidence,
research on dust clouds of Mars seemed to fit with their fire
studies. When the U.S. Mariner 9 spacecraft began to orbit
Mars in 1971, it sent back photographs of a planet shrouded
in dust that had been stirred up by high winds. As the storm
ended and fine particles settled back to the Martian surface,
scientists were able to measure temperature changes on Mars.
Calculations showed that the dust had absorbed sunlight and
had warmed the upper atmosphere, but the Martian land
surface had become chilled. Such dust storms and temperature
changes are common on Mars.

In the early 1980s, many scientists became interested in the
climatic effects of dust clouds on earth. Paleontologists were
curious because of a new theory that the extinction of dinosaurs
had been caused by dust clouds raised by the collision of an
asteroid with the earth. Astronomer Carl Sagan of Cornell
University and his colleagues decided to apply knowledge
gained from observations of Martian dust clouds to the earth's
atmosphere: "We calculated by how much the Earth's global
temperature should decline after a major volcanic explosion
and found that our results (generally a fraction of a degree)
were in good accord with actual measurements," wrote Sagan.
The 1815 eruption of an Indonesian volcano lowered global
temperatures by about 2° Fahrenheit, resulting in "the year
without a summer" in 1816, when many crops failed to ripen.

Upon reading the *Ambio* report of Birks and Crutzen, Sagan
and other scientists decided to apply their findings about dust

clouds and climatic changes to the effects of a nuclear war. His colleagues were California research scientist Richard Turco and three atmospheric scientists at the National Aeronautics and Space Administration's Ames Research Center in California— Brian Toon, Thomas Ackerman, and James Pollack. Their study, published in 1983, became known as the TTAPS report (the acronym represents the first letters of their last names).

The TTAPS team used computer models to investigate the impact of different amounts of dust, fine soil particles, smoke, and other matter in the atmosphere. They made careful assumptions about such factors as fire size, duration of burning, heights of smoke plumes, and the optical qualities of dust and soot (dust scatters light, soot absorbs it). These assumptions were fed into a computer with 40 different scenarios of nuclear wars, ranging from the use of 100 megatons (the equivalent of 8,000 Hiroshima bombs) to 10,000 megatons.

"Our baseline case, as in many other studies," wrote Sagan, "was a 5,000-megaton war with only a modest fraction of the yield (20 percent) expended on urban or industrial targets. Our job, in each case, was to follow the dust and smoke generated, see how much sunlight was absorbed and by how much the temperatures changed, figure out how the particles spread in longitude and latitude, and calculate how long before it all fell out of the air back onto the surface.

"The results of our calculations astonished us," Sagan continued, "In the baseline case, the amount of sunlight at the ground was reduced to a few percent of normal—much darker, in daylight, than in a heavy overcast and too dark for plants to make a living from photosynthesis. At least in the Northern Hemisphere, where the great preponderance of strategic targets lies, an unbroken and deadly gloom would persist for weeks.

"Even more unexpected were the temperatures calculated. In the baseline case, land temperatures, except for narrow strips of coastline, dropped to minus 13° Fahrenheit and stayed below freezing for months—even for a summer war . . . . The oceans, a significant heat reservoir, would not freeze, however, and a major ice age would probably not be triggered. But because the temperatures would drop so catastrophically, virtually all crops and farm animals, at least in the Northern Hemisphere, would be destroyed, as would most varieties of uncultivated or undomesticated food supplies. Most of the human survivors would starve."

According to the TTAPS study, disturbance of the earth's normal climate would create new weather patterns. The sharp temperature difference between land and ocean waters would produce fairly constant storms along the East, West, and Gulf coasts, with gale-force winds. More important, evidence suggests that the usual separation of Northern and Southern Hemisphere air circulation might be broken, and hundreds of tons of soot, dust, and radioactive debris might be carried into the Southern Hemisphere.

Perhaps the most unexpected and disturbing TTAPS finding was the climatic changes resulting from a scenario of a "small" nuclear war of 100 megatons. Warheads were airburst over a hundred cities, and the resulting fires and fires storms produced a dark, cold pall over the Northern Hemisphere almost as harsh as in the 5,000-megaton case. If the assumptions of the TTAPS computer studies are correct, the explosion of less than 1 percent of the world's strategic nuclear arsenals will produce what Richard Turco has called the nuclear winter.

If the assumptions are correct—that is a big "if." The old saying about computer studies—"garbage in, garbage out"— still holds; results are no better than the data upon which they are based. Our attempts to make computer models of the earth's climate are still at a rather elementary level. In 1984, Harvard biologist Stephen Jay Gould listed some of the difficulties: "We

The amount of smoke reaching the atmosphere, its height, and its duration aloft are key unknowns in the hypothetical nuclear winter, but it is judged to be a clear possibility by many scientists.

must deal . . . with a score of variables whose values we cannot specify exactly and whose interactions are largely unknown since the experiment, thank God, has not been tried. How much dust and soot goes up; does it spread to a homogeneous layer or does it leave holes for intermittent sunlight; does it spread to the Southern Hemisphere and, if so, how intensely; where in the atmosphere do dust and soot lodge and how long will they stay before rains scavenge the particles and bring them to earth; how cold will it get; how long will the effects last? I could go on forever but will stop here. And these are only the first-order questions about unknown immediate effects."

Some assumptions and conclusions of the TTAPS study have been criticized. In particular, the idea that we know enough to set 100 megatons as the threshold of nuclear winter has been questioned. Some critics scoffed at the entire TTAPS study, saying, "We can't predict the weather two weeks from today, so how can we possibly understand the meteorology of nuclear war?"

According to Stephen Schneider of the National Center for Atmospheric Research in Colorado, this argument is a red herring, since the TTAPS study dealt with climate, not weather. Speaking at the 1984 meeting of the American Association for the Advancement of Science, Schneider said, "We can predict climate. It will be hot this summer and cold this winter, and we know why. We can do large-scale climatic projections, and nuclear war is large-scale."

Using a far more sophisticated computer model than that of the TTAPS study, Schneider and his colleagues found that they differed about some details but agreed with the basic TTAPS findings. About the TTAPS research, an atmospheric scientist at California's Lawrence Livermore National Laboratory said, "We ran their baseline study through our computers, as well as our own war scenarios, and some of their assumptions are debatable. But changing them wouldn't make the problem go away—there would be profound climatic changes if we had a big war and a lot of cities were burned."

Scientists agree that nuclear war would cause some climatic change, but disagree about its severity. The TTAPS study stimulated dozens of meetings and further research on the climate after nuclear war. In April 1983, forty biologists met in Massachusetts to analyze the ecological implications if a nuclear winter occurred after a 5,000-megaton war, as described in the TTAPS report. Their findings, entitled "Long-term Biological Consequences of Nuclear War," were published in *Science* magazine.

The biologists concluded that human starvation would occur in the Southern Hemisphere, not only because of a lack of imported food from the north, but also because of cold air killing delicate tropical growth, causing mass extinction of many plants and animals. In the Northern Hemisphere, the cold, the year-round frozen lakes, and lack of food would also cause many species to die out.

Inevitably the question of human extinction arose. This seemed unlikely, at least immediately, according to the biologists, who then wrote, "Whether any people would be able to persist for long in the face of highly modified biological communities; novel climates; high levels of radiation; shattered agricultural, social, and economic systems; extraordinary psychological stresses; and a host of other difficulties is open to question. It is clear that the ecosystem effects *alone* resulting from a large-scale thermonuclear war could be enough to destroy the current civilization in at least the Northern Hemisphere." The biologists noted that the war scenario they studied was by no means the largest war possible, so "the possibility of the extinction of *Homo sapiens* cannot be excluded."

In December 1984 a study group of the National Academy of Sciences reported that despite the limitations of computer models, nuclear winter in the Northern Hemisphere was a "clear possibility."

The TTAPS study stimulated a wave of research on climatic and chemical processes that could be set off by nuclear explosions. These new studies may or may not establish that nuclear winter is a strong possibility. Computer models of global atmospheric patterns, as sophisticated as they are, still leave plenty of room for doubt.

There are so many unknowns about such a war, and so few are testable. Since long-range missiles are expensive, they are tested much less than other kinds of arms. No silo has ever been struck by a nuclear warhead to test the effectiveness of either. Since nearly all nations honor the ban on aboveground nuclear bursts, deep underground explosions have to suffice. The nuclear test ban treaty also means that tests of protective measures against EMP must be simulated. And these are some of the technological devices that are truly testable, unlike many other aspects, such as human behavior in nuclear war, about which we can make only assumptions.

The physicist Freeman Dyson wrote in *Weapons and Hope* that such studies as the *Ambio* project and TTAPS nuclear winter research are important even if one does not agree with their conclusions. They are based on many unproved assumptions, all open to challenge. These studies do not actually make our knowledge of the effects of nuclear war more precise. In Dyson's opinion, they are important for the opposite reason— they show that our ignorance is even greater than anyone realized. We continue to uncover more and more unpleasant possibilities.

Such studies have, Dyson believes, "confirmed in the present era the judgment that Tolstoy expressed in *War and Peace* a century ago: that war is in its nature incalculable and unpredictable and uncontrollable."

Human curiosity is strong, but nuclear war is not a fit subject for experimentation. There's very little we can learn until it is too late, until the weapons have been used. What we have learned, together with our unproved assumptions, strongly suggests that the nation that starts nuclear war will be making a murder-suicide pact with its opponent and threatening every living thing on earth. That is knowledge enough, and a powerful incentive for people to work to ensure that all of the rest remains forever a mystery.

# Glossary

**alpha rays**—charged particles, made up of two protons and two neutrons, which are emitted from the nucleus of a radioactive atom. Although alpha rays cannot penetrate the skin, once inhaled or swallowed these slow-moving particles can cause great harm.

**atom**—the smallest unit of an element, consisting of a central nucleus surrounded by orbiting electrons, which has all of the characteristics of that element.

**beta rays**—high-energy electrons emitted from the nucleus of a radioactive atom. They travel almost as fast as the speed of light and can penetrate human flesh.

**blast wave**—a pulse of air pressure that spreads outward in all directions from an explosion. Blast waves of nuclear explosions are so powerful that they induce winds of several hundred miles an hour.

**chain reaction**—a self-sustaining nuclear reaction that occurs when a neutron splits an atom, releasing further neutrons, which cause still more atoms to split and emit more neutrons, and so on.

**circular error probable (CEP)**—an estimate of missile accuracy, CEP is the radius of a circle around a target in which half of the missiles aimed at the target would land.

**counterforce attack**—an attack aimed at an enemy's military forces, including submarine and air bases, missile silos, and command and communication facilities.

**critical mass**—the smallest amount of fissionable material, such as uranium, needed to sustain a nuclear chain reaction.

**deuterium**—an isotope or form of hydrogen in which the nucleus contains a proton and a neutron rather than simply a proton. In nuclear warheads, deuterium reacts with tritium to produce a fusion reaction.

**electron**—a negatively charged particle of an atom that orbits its nucleus. Emitted by radioactive substances, electrons are called beta rays or beta particles.

**electromagnetic pulse**—a burst of electrical energy caused by exploding a nuclear weapon high in the atmosphere. It is similar to lightning but represents a rise in voltage a hundred times as fast, capable of doing great harm to electrical and electronic devices and systems.

**fallout**—radioactive particles that are carried into the upper atmosphere by a nuclear explosion and that eventually fall back to the earth's surface.

**fission**—the process by which an atomic nucleus of a heavy atom splits and produces heat energy and radioactive particles.

**fratricide**—the destruction or disablement of incoming missiles caused by the effects of explosions of preceding missiles.

**fusion**—the process by which lightweight atomic nuclei are joined, forming heavier elements and producing energy.

**gamma rays**—high-energy radiation of great penetrating power, emitted from the nuclei of some radioactive elements. Similar to x-rays, gamma rays require heavy shielding, such as lead or brick, to stop them.

**ground zero**—the point on the ground where a nuclear weapon explodes, or the point directly beneath an airburst nuclear weapon.

**hibakusha**—"explosion-affected persons"—the survivors of nuclear explosions at Hiroshima and Nagasaki.

**hydrogen bomb**—a nuclear weapon in which part of the explosive energy is a result of fusion. Forms of hydrogen are the ingredients of the fusion reaction.

**ionizing radiation**—types of radiation that are powerful enough to cause electrons to be emitted from atoms or to be added to them, thus producing ions with either a positive or negative charge. Ionizing radiation includes neutrons, x-rays, gamma rays, beta rays, and cosmic rays.

**isotopes**—forms of the same element having identical chemical characteristics but having different numbers of neutrons in their nuclei. The element hydrogen has three isotopes.

**kiloton**—an explosive force equal to that of 1,000 tons of TNT.

**leukemia**—cancer of the blood. A disease of the tissues that produce white blood cells, which causes an excess of abnormal blood cells.

**multiple independently targetable reentry vehicle (MIRV)**—a missile carrying two or more warheads, each of which can be aimed at a different target.

**neutron**—a particle of an atomic nucleus with no electrical charge. Neutrons are emitted at high speed during fission and can be absorbed by other nuclei.

**neutron bomb**—a small thermonuclear weapon designed to produce less blast and more neutron radiation than normal. Its effects would not be much different from other thermonuclear weapons of equal strength, though its neutrons would kill or injure more people and its blast would cause less damage.

**nucleus**—the central, positively charged part of an atom, made up of protons and neutrons (with the exception of ordinary hydrogen, which has no neutron).

**overpressure**—the amount by which the blast wave of a nuclear explosion exceeds the normal atmospheric pressure, which is 14.7 pounds per square inch at sea level.

**proton**—a positively charged particle that makes up part of the nucleus of an atom.

**radioactivity**—the property of some elements, such as uranium, of spontaneously emitting alpha, beta, or gamma rays. About fifty elements are naturally radioactive; radioactivity can also be produced artificially.

**rad**—a unit of ionizing radiation that is actually absorbed by living tissues. Rad stands for "*r*adiation *a*bsorbed *d*ose."

**rem**—a unit of ionizing radiation that is capable of causing a particular amount of damage to human cells. It stands for "*r*oentgen *e*quivalent *m*an."

**shroud**—the metal shield that covers the tip of a MIRV missile and protects warheads and the postboost vehicle during the boost phase of the missile's flight.

**strategic nuclear weapons**—weapons that can strike very distant targets and therefore are delivered by long-range bombers or long-range missiles.

**tactical nuclear weapons**—weapons that can strike targets in a particular region or theater, delivered by short- or intermediate-range missiles or airplanes or by such battlefield weapons as artillery.

**thermonuclear weapons**—nuclear weapons in which fusion reactions take place. Temperatures of several million degrees are required for fusion to occur.

**triad**—a strategic nuclear force composed of long-range bombers, land-launched missiles, and sea-launched missiles.

**tritium**—an isotope or form of hydrogen having a proton and two neutrons in its nucleus. In thermonuclear weapons, tritium reacts with deuterium to produce a fusion reaction.

**uranium**—a dark gray metal that is the heaviest element to occur naturally. The isotope uranium-235 is the fuel of reactors in nuclear electric-generating plants. Uranium-238 produces about half of the explosive yield of a thermonuclear weapon.

# Further Reading

BOOKS AND REPORTS

Adams, Ruth, and Cullen, Susan, editors. *The Final Epidemic: Physicians and Scientists on Nuclear War*. Chicago: Educational Foundation for Nuclear Science, 1981.

Akizuki, Tatsuichiro, *Nagasaki 1945*. London: Quartet Books, 1981.

British Medical Association. *The Medical Effects of Nuclear War*. Report of the British Medical Association's Board of Science and Education. New York: Wiley, 1983.

Cassel, C., McCally, M., and Abraham, H., editors. *Nuclear Weapons and Nuclear War: A Source Book for Health Professionals*. New York: Praeger, 1984.

Clark, Ronald. *The Greatest Power on Earth*. New York: Harper and Row, 1980.

Clark, Wilson, and Page, Jake. *Energy, Vulnerability and War*. New York: W.W. Norton, 1981.

Committee for the Compilation of Materials on Damage Caused by the Atomic Bombs in Hiroshima and Nagasaki. *Hiroshima and Nagasaki: The Physical, Medical, and Social Effects of the Atomic Bombings*. New York: Basic Books, Inc., 1981.

Dyson, Freeman. *Weapons and Hope*. New York: Harper and Row, 1984.

Ehrlich, Paul R., et al. *The Cold and the Dark: The World After Nuclear War*. New York: W.W. Norton, 1984.

Glasstone, S., and Dolen, P., editors. *Effects of Nuclear Weapons*, third edition. Washington, D.C.: U.S. Department of Defense and Department of Energy, 1977.

Goodwin, Peter. *Nuclear War: The Facts on Our Survival*. New York: Rutledge Press, 1981.

Ground Zero Staff. *Nuclear War: What's In It for You?* New York: Pocket Books, 1982.

Harwell, Mark. *Nuclear Winter: The Human and Environmental Consequences of Nuclear War*. New York: Springer-Verlag, 1984.

Hersey, John. *Hiroshima*. New York: Knopf, 1946.

Katz, Arthur. *Life After Nuclear War*. Cambridge, Mass.: Ballinger Publishing Company, 1982.

National Research Council Committee on the Atmospheric Effects of Nuclear Explosions. *The Effects on the Atmosphere of a Major Nuclear Exchange*. Washington, D.C.: National Academy Press, 1985.

Office of Technology Assessment. *The Effects of Nuclear War*. Washington, D.C.: U.S. Government Printing Office, 1979.

Osada, Arata. *Children of Hiroshima*. New York: Harper and Row, 1982.

Peterson, Jeannie, editor. *The Aftermath: The Human and Ecological Consequences of Nuclear War*. (Based on a special issue of *Ambio*.) New York: Pantheon Books, 1983.

Pringle, Laurence. *Radiation: Waves and Particles/Benefits and Risks*. Hillside, New Jersey: Enslow Publishers, Inc., 1983.

Russett, Bruce. *The Prisoners of Insecurity*. San Francisco: W.H. Freeman, 1983.

Schell, Jonathan. *The Fate of the Earth*. New York: Knopf, 1982.

Szasz, Ferenc. *The Day the Sun Rose Twice: The Story of the Trinity Site Nuclear Explosion July 16, 1945*. Albuquerque: University of New Mexico Press, 1984.

Tsipis, Kosta. *Arsenal: Understanding Weapons in the Nuclear Age*. New York: Simon and Schuster, 1983.

U.S. Arms Control and Disarmament Agency. *An Analysis of Civil Defense in Nuclear War*. Washington, D.C.: Arms Control and Disarmament Agency, 1978.

Zuckerman, Edward. *The Day After World War III*. New York: Viking Press, 1984.

## PERIODICALS

Bernstein, Barton. "Truman and the H-Bomb." *Bulletin of the Atomic Scientists*, March 1984, pp. 12-18.

——. "The Unsung Father of the A-Bomb." *Discover*, August 1985, pp. 36-42.

Bunn, Matthew, and Tsipis, Kosta. "The Uncertainties of a Pre-emptive Nuclear Attack." *Scientific American*, November 1983, pp. 38-47.

Drell, Sidney, and von Hippel, Frank. "Limited Nuclear War." *Scientific American*, November 1976, pp. 27-37.

Ehrlich, Anne. "Nuclear Winter: A Forecast of the Climatic and Biological Effects of Nuclear War." *Bulletin of the Atomic Scientists*, April 1984 (special 16-page insert).

Gottfried, Kurt, *et al.* "'No First Use' of Nuclear Weapons." *Scientific American*, March 1984, pp. 33-41.

Kaplan, F.M. "The Soviet Civil Defense Myth, Parts 1 and 2." *Bulletin of the Atomic Scientists*, March and April 1978.

Levi, Barbara. "Atmospheric Calculations Suggest a Nuclear Winter." *Physics Today*, February 1984, pp. 17-20.

——. "The Nuclear Arsenals of the US and USSR." *Physics Today*, March 1983, pp. 43-49.

Maddox, John. "Nuclear Winter Not Yet Established." *Nature*, March 1, 1984, p. 11.

Mohs, Mayo. "America's 50th Biggest Business." *Discover*, August 1985, pp. 24-35.

Morrison, David. "ICBM Vulnerability." *Bulletin of the Atomic Scientists*, November 1984, pp. 22-29.

Overbye, Dennis. "Prophet of the Cold and Dark" (Scientist of the Year Paul Crutzen). *Discover*, January 1985, pp. 24-32.

Sartori, Leo. "When the Bomb Falls," the Weapons Tutorial, Part 5. *Bulletin of the Atomic Scientists*, June-July 1983, pp. 40-47.

Steinbruner, John. "Launch Under Attack." *Scientific American*, January 1984, pp. 37-47.

Takahashi, Shinji. "Relief for the Hibakusha." *Bulletin of the Atomic Scientists*, October 1984, pp. 25-26.

Turco, R., Toon, O., Ackerman, T., Pollack, J., and Sagan, C. "Nuclear Winter: Global Consequences of Multiple Nuclear Explosions." *Science*, December 23, 1983, pp. 1283-1292.

von Hippel, Frank. "The Myths of Edward Teller." *Bulletin of the Atomic Scientists*, March 1983, pp. 6-12.

Winkler, Allan. "A 40-Year History of Civil Defense." *Bulletin of the Atomic Scientists*, June-July 1984, pp. 16-22.

# Index